★ THE ★

SOUTHERN

ADVANTAGE

WHY YOU SHOULD CONSIDER
DOING BUSINESS IN THE WORLD'S
FOURTH-LARGEST ECONOMY

★ THE ★
SOUTHERN
ADVANTAGE

JOE HOLLINGSWORTH, JR.
WITH MIKE RANDLE AND TRISHA OSTROWSKI

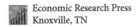

Economic Research Press
Knoxville, TN

Published by Economic Research Press
200 Prosperity Drive
Suite 126
Knoxville, TN 37923

Publisher's Cataloging-in-Publication Data
Hollingsworth, Jr., Joe

The Southern advantage: why you should consider doing business in the world's fourth largest economy / Joe Hollingsworth, Jr.—Knoxville, TN : Economic Research Press, 2003

p. ; cm.
ISBN: 0-9743941-0-6

1. Southern States—Economic conditions. 2. Business—Southern States. 3. Southern States—History. 4. Southern States—Social life and customs. I. Title.

| HC107 .A13 H65 | 2003 | 2003110344 |
| 330/.0975 | —dc22 | 0308 |

Project coordination by Jenkins Group, Inc. · www.bookpublishing.com
Cover design by Chris Rhoads
Interior design by Paw Print Media
For order information, please visit www.thesouthernadvantage.com

Printed in the United States of America

07 06 05 04 03 · 5 4 3 2 1

Contents

Thanks Page ...   vii

one   The World's Fourth Largest Economy   1

two   Down Home   19

three   Where We Came From   27

four   The Tide Starts to Turn   41

five   The "Sunbelt" Rises   55

six   The Migration Peaks   67

seven   As the South Matures   81

eight   Population Explosion   95

nine   Southern Leaders   111

ten   Crunch the Numbers   133

eleven   Five of the Most Important Reasons
           You Should Expand Your Business
           to the South . . .   147

twelve   Quality of Life Does Matter!   161

           Predictions, Projections, and Trends   175

           The Final Word . . .   201

Thanks Page ...

I had to ask myself, why in the world would anyone write a book like this and the reasons why they shouldn't were apparent. . . .

1. First of all, there is the "obvious" that not everybody is going to be interested in the economic destiny of a region.
2. If they are interested, they are probably so busy they haven't got time to sit down and read this book (reminds me of the old adage that "I am too busy earning a living to make any real money").
3. Then how do you get the word out about the book? That will involve a lot of personal time.

If the absolutely absurd happens and we should actually make a profit, it will surprise everybody. So if we accomplish the absurd, then we will donate 50 percent of the profits to the Southern Economic Development Council (SEDC) to encourage our Southern message to be broadcast even further.

But the book NEEDS to be written because the story needs to be told. I have searched the bookshelves and I can't find any volume that has truly addressed the progress the South has made. So this will be our humble attempt to get the message out.

An interesting occurence happened during the final days before the launch of the book. While in New York to explain the benefits of The South to key players in the public relations field, the famous northeast "blackout" occurred due to an antiquated electrical grid. It seemed like the height of irony and possibly a good omen for the book. To be explaining the many southern advantages when the lights went out was most entertaining! Most certainly it was a wake-up call for our friends in the northeast.

Now I need to thank the folks who have been so supportive and helpful during the many inconvenient hours of work on this book.

My first thanks are to my family, who always turn out to be my cheerleaders. My wife of 22 years, Marsha, our son, Trey, who is currently at the Wharton Business School, and daughter Nicci, who is graduating from high school and of course, my father, Joe Hollingsworth, Sr., and my mother, the late Mary Claiborne Hollingsworth. Without their support and love, I could not have devoted the time necessary to this endeavor.

▶ I want to say that I have an incredible staff at the Hollingsworth Companies! I never cease to be amazed at the number of people who can step up and perform at a higher level of achievement when they are encouraged to do so. Our staff has done so while I have been consumed writing this book. Without listing everybody's name specifically, it is with untiring appreciation and pride that I congratulate you all on simply being a "world-class" team. Your level of excellence pushes my envelope every day.

▶ It is amazing how many people actually contribute to the thoughts and direction of such an undertaking. While I am certainly no believer in decisions by committees or "paralysis through analysis," the suggestions of others were not only valuable but in many cases helped to better formulate the general concepts with which we began. These people have been too numerous to mention, but they have contributed significantly to the outcome. I must mention four individuals who contributed to the book and then assisted with the final edit. David Dodd of Dadco Consulting Services, Inc., of Shreveport, La., Bob Goforth and Bob Leak of Goforth and Leak Consulting of Raleigh, North Carolina/Jacksonville, Florida, and Jim Clinton of the Southern Growth Policy Board, also in North Carolina. Their efforts and encouragement were extremely important to me.

▶ When there simply was no book available like this and not knowing if there was a market for it or if anybody cared, two people stepped up to whom I will forever be indebted. The first is Mike Randle, the founder and publisher of *Southern Business and Development.* Mike has to be recognized for his amazing knowledge of the South and his enthusiastic support for the Southern economic success story. He knows more about the South's individual communities and their success pattern than anybody in the business. Trisha Ostrowski, managing editor for the same magazine, is one of those rare individuals who can have a page completely written while you think you are just chatting on the phone with her. Much of the research and writing have fallen on Trisha's shoulders and she should forever be proud of her contribution.

We have done our absolute best to make sure we were clear on each fact. But in all economic discussions there is a chance for statistical misunderstandings. So if anything like that crops up here, I would be happy to be of service. Feel free to contact me by email at *jhollingsworth@hollingsworthcos.com*.

one

The World's Fourth Largest Economy

I t has been called the "locomotive powering the nation's economy."

Today, the American South is not only vibrant and dynamic; it is also highly industrialized and becoming a magnet for in-migration and business investment from all parts of the globe. Since the 1980s, the region has achieved record prosperity as it continues to outpace the nation in nearly every economic indicator.

Journalist Peter Appleborne has made a convincing case in *Dixie Rising* that the South has finally put defeat in the Civil War behind it and is now a "rising" region that is shaping American values, politics, and culture.

With such phenomenal growth, the South has come extremely far in an incredibly short period of time—essentially one generation. Dixie has picked itself up by its bootstraps and has fully transformed its economy through industrialization, urban growth, establishment of higher quality of life opportunities, and the pursuit of equality for all races.

"Array the major regions of the United States on whatever economic, demographic, political or cultural variable you wish, and usually the South (in the past) stood alone at one end of the continuum. Sometimes the Northeast occupied the other end, sometimes the West, but almost invariably, you found the South out there on its own: less wealthy, less healthy, more rural, more religious, more pessimistic, more conservative, less 'American' than the other regions," John Reed Shelton of the Roper Center explained about the region's past in "The South's Three Personas."

But if the South has most often been the exception to the "American rule," it has in the past 50 years started to contradict this historic perception. Bear in mind that the South now leads the nation in total population, job creation, and virtually every other economic category. It is the most industrialized part of the nation with eight of the top ten states in terms of manufacturing growth located in this region.

Once the land of agriculture and textiles, in today's South the people making industrial machinery and electronic equipment substantially outnumber those producing textiles or sewing apparel. Automobile and printing plants virtually equal textile mills as sources of employment. Also in the last five decades, the number of people employed in agriculture has dropped from nearly half to less than five percent of the South's total workforce.

The South's cities today are places of vibrant energy and boundless confidence linked by high-tech commerce and communication. Atlanta, for example, is home to the world-changing CNN 24-hour news network, the world's biggest soft drink company, and one of the world's busiest airports. Charlotte is among the biggest financial centers in terms of banking assets. Dallas-

Ft. Worth is practically the center of the North American universe. Memphis has become America's distribution capital. Midsize as well as smaller cities have also mushroomed. Two out of three Southerners are now urban or suburban dwellers and even in rural areas, many people work in industry.

For good reason, individuals and companies are beating a path to the South's door.

Searching for a better life and a better living, individuals from young professionals to retirees are recognizing the *Southern advantage* like never before. Millions of people have moved to the South from the nation and the world. Formerly "less wealthy" than other areas, personal income in the South is now more than 90 percent of the national average with prevailing trends headed upward. And with the lower cost of living and taxation (when compared to other sections of the country), Southerners can enjoy a much higher level of affluence. The South has achieved a whole new level of popularity—with native-born Southerners, with self-proclaimed Southerners (also known as transplants), and with people who are returning after pursuing opportunity in other regions.

For businesses on the fast track, a Southern location enables companies across most every channel or sector to find the type of success they've never experienced—the kind that happens quicker, lasts longer, and costs less. A wealth of advantages such as reduced tax burdens, lower operating costs, a great work ethic, outstanding training programs, and the predominance of Right-to-Work protections are attracting all sizes of companies in record numbers.

In fact, the question for most companies is no longer whether they should locate in the South; it's whether they can afford not to!

Attesting to the South's benefits are scores of homegrown companies. Among the market leaders that have grown up in the region are Delta Airlines, CNN, FedEx, Dell, and Compaq. Even the world's number-one company, based on 2002 revenues, Wal-Mart, was born and bred in the South. The decidedly business-friendly climate has also attracted foreign investment from companies like BMW, Mercedes, Nissan, Toyota, and Hyundai. This in addition to attracting the headquarters of entrenched Northern presence firms like American Airlines, J.C. Penney, and UPS.

While the South's rise to greatness may surprise those who thought of the region as unsophisticated or backwoods, Southerners have worked diligently to dispel that perception by aggressively pursuing economic expansion as well as opportunity in any form. During the last 50 years every wall that stood between the American South and economic prominence has been demolished not with the swiftness of the Berlin Wall but with patience and perseverance that were the result of pure determination. The region has finally shed the baggage that weighed it down for so long and the pace of change is quickening as the South moves onto the world economic scene as a sizeable force of value and viability. Perhaps most stunning, the American South is now considered the world's fourth-largest economy (behind the U.S. as a whole, Japan, and Germany).

What I'd like to "drop" on you now I call the South's "bombshells." These economic and social accomplishments powerfully dispel the longtime misconceptions about the South—perhaps even some that you've personally held. They will help you gain the full picture of how far the region has come. They also serve as a testament that the Southern region of the U.S. is one of the most attractive places to live and work on the planet.

Now for the bombshells:

Bombshell #1
The South has doubled its population in only 30 years

Many people don't realize how fast the South has grown. We continue to experience an in-migration of folks from all parts of the world; "imports" as we often refer to them.

Right after World War II, the South, Northeast, and Midwest all had about the same population. In fact, the 1950 U.S. Census shows that the Midwest had a population of 44.6 million, the Northeast 42.3 million, and the South 43.3 million. In 1950, the West was the only region that was not comparable. It had a population of just 19.4 million.

As of 2001, according to the U.S. Census the Midwest and Northeast each had a population of around 55.5 million. In just 52 years, the West has shot past those two regions with 63 million persons. The South's population growth in 50 years has been extraordinary. In 2001, the South had a population of 107 million persons, or about the same as the population of the Midwest and Northeast combined.

The reason for this population explosion? America can't seem to get enough of the South—from its weather to its music to its cooking. Census Bureau statistics indicate that more Americans will migrate to the South in coming years than to any other region of the country. Interregional migration currently happens more often in the South as the thriving economy attracts non-Southerners and out-migration has slowed.

Until recently, most people who lived in the South were born there; but now the South has used its warm hospitality and quality of living to attract newcomers, proving itself as an appealing place to put down roots. As we enter the twenty-first century, larger and larger numbers of Southern residents were born outside the South. Texas has now surpassed New York as the second most populous state with Florida not far behind.

The South's population explosion has been due in large part to two crucial inventions. 1)The air conditioner, which has made the summers tolerable. 2) The mechanized cotton-picker, that removed the need for cheap agricultural labor and prompted Southern state governments to relentlessly recruit industry to employ their people. Additionally, you can't discount the value of Southern hospitality in attracting population growth. Studies have found that Southerners more often smile at strangers, are more likely to help a blind person cross the street, and are more likely to pick up someone's dropped coin and hand it back to them.

Bombshell #2
The South currently holds the top spot in EVERY 'Gross Regional Product' category

In 1996, the American South topped the Northeast, Midwest, and West in every Gross Regional Product category identified by the federal government but one. The South led all regions in the value of production in manufacturing, construction, farms/forestry, transportation, wholesale trade, retail trade, and government categories. The only category where the South did not outperform all other U.S. regions was the FIRE sector (finances, insurance, and real estate).

But that changed in 2000, when the South produced a FIRE GRP of $250.6 billion, while the Northeast's total was $248 billion that year. What this means is that the South leads all U.S. regions in every Gross Regional Product category, something I'm sure Franklin Roosevelt couldn't even have imagined when he

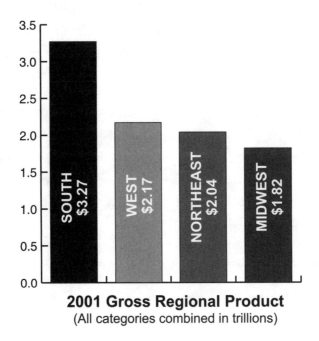

2001 Gross Regional Product
(All categories combined in trillions)

Source: U.S. Statistical Abstract 2002

launched the New Deal and the Tennessee Valley Authority in the 1930s in an effort to "prime the pump of the most impoverished region of this great nation."

Bombshell #3
The South leads the nation in job creation

If you are looking for a job, nowhere else in the country has a more plentiful supply than the South. From 1992-2001, the United States saw the creation of 22,015,000 net new jobs. That's an astounding figure, a 10-year total that can't be rivaled in the history of the nation's economy. The South's contribution to the total number of jobs created in this country over the last 10 years is even more astounding. From 1992-2001, the South has created 10,146,000 net new jobs. That means roughly half of all the jobs created nationwide during the 1990s were created in the South.

It's important to note here that these job-creation figures are especially impressive in light of my observation that the South is bearing the brunt of the impact of the North American Free Trade Agreement (NAFTA). The region has lost more than its share of jobs as manufacturers have moved to Mexico in search of pennies-on-the-dollar wage rates which no U.S.-based operator can match.

Even in a challenging economy, the South appears to be less hard hit than other regions in terms of jobs. As America entered

Job Creation in Southern States — Last 10 Years
(net new jobs by state)

Source: U.S. Bureau of Labor Statistics 2002

the twenty-first century things were tough all over, but the South once again continues to buck this trend. A set of Labor Department data aptly named JOLTS, for job openings and labor turnover statistics, reveals that between mid-2001 and May 2002, job openings in the Northeast fell by 250,000, or about 29 percent. The Midwest fared even worse, with job openings plunging by 313,000, or 31 percent, during the same period. The South shone by comparison, since it had the most job openings to start with (1.5 million) and lost the fewest (122,000, or about 8 percent).

The South was led by Texas, which created a net new job total of 2,349,000 between 1992 and 2001. Florida is the South's second largest generator of jobs over the last 10 years with 1,689,000. Georgia created an even 1,000,000 and North Carolina came in with 829,000 net new jobs since 1992.

Bombshell #4
When it comes to education levels, the South is on course to surpass all other regions

Over the last 10 years, the South has made significant gains on the national averages in educational attainment.

For comparison, let's look at 1992. That year, the U.S. average of high school graduates was at 75.2 percent. Meanwhile, the South's average high school graduate rate was nearly five points behind the U.S. average, at 70.8 percent.

Today, the gains the South has made in educational attainment are readily apparent. In 2001, the national high school graduation rate was 84.1 percent. Now, less than two points behind is the South's high school graduation rate of 82.2 percent. This figure represents nearly a three-point gain in 10 years.

Mirroring the increase in high school educational attainment in the South is the rise in the number of Southerners who hold college degrees of four years or more. The current U.S. average is 25.6 percent. The current average in the South of residents with four-year degrees or more is 23 percent, or a scant 2.6 percent difference from the U.S. average. This rise in college-educated Southerners has produced a large base of independent thinkers and innovators.

The increase in educational attainment in select Southern states since World War II is tracked by The Southern Regional Education Board (SREB). SREB was founded in 1948 at the request of Southern leaders in business, education, and government. Reflective of how serious the South has been about improving its education levels, SREB was the nation's first compact for education. Over the years it has worked to improve every aspect of education from early childhood education to doctoral degrees and beyond.

Bombshell #5
The South has one of the lowest African-American poverty rates and is the leading region for in-migration of this ethnic group

When embarking on this research, we tried to find poverty rates for African-Americans in 1963, the year that Martin Luther King gave his "I have a dream" speech at the Lincoln Memorial. This speech was pivotal in that it clearly brought to the world's attention the plight of the African-American segment of our population. To me, 1963 was a natural baseline. Shockingly, no data exists from which to study trending. The federal government didn't begin tracking African-American poverty until 1966, even though white poverty had been tracked with some accuracy since the 1930s. In 1966, 42 percent of African-Americans in the U.S. were at or below the poverty level. While I could find no state data which would give me a Southern percentage of African-American poverty, one could easily estimate that such poverty in the South was at least 20 percentage points higher than the national average.

In 1992, poverty levels of African-Americans in the South remained alarmingly high at about one in three. But since 1992, such poverty in the American South has dropped dramatically. In 1994, for the first time ever, African-Americans in the South were faring better than those in the Midwest and about the same as those in the Northeast in terms of poverty rates. Jump to 2002, and 21 percent of African-American Southerners are at or below the poverty level. That figure is, for the first time in history, lower than other regions of the U.S. In fact, African-American poverty in the Northeast (22.5 percent) and Midwest (24.4 percent) is higher than that found in the South. These figures don't even account for the lower cost of living in the South, which could subtract another two percentage points!

The South was the part of America where slavery lasted longest and died hardest. Now, the region attracts African-Americans in huge numbers. Its schools are less segregated and more African-Americans hold public office here than anywhere else in the country. With half of the U.S. African-American population, the South now elects a large percentage of African-Americans as public office holders. For businesses looking to set up shop in the South, if you hear that the South is a bastion of African-American poverty, don't believe it. African-American Southerners have picked themselves up in the last four decades and are surpassing their brothers and sisters to the North in personal and household gains. The facts (U.S. Census Bureau) are hard to dispute.

Bombshell #6
Diversity is ALIVE! The Southern stereotype is dying!

In just the last 10 years, many born-and-raised Southerners, especially those in rural areas, small markets, and mid-markets, have grown accustomed to seeing folks from different countries at the most popular restaurant in town, speaking a language other than English. Ten years ago, this was an initial shock to many of those Southerners. Today, it is routine.

In larger markets but not the South's largest, such as Birmingham, Greenville, Jacksonville, Memphis, San Antonio, Louisville, and Richmond for example, the languages and accents heard and spoken over the last 10 years have changed from a Southern drawl almost exclusively. Now you hear a myriad of dialects from New Yorkese to Bostonian, to those strange sounds that come forth from the mouths of folks from the U.S.A.'s Great White North "Minnesewta and WisCahnsin." Throw in Asian, African, Middle Eastern, and Spanish influences and the South's most important markets for the next decade have now earned their diversity degrees just since the early 1990s.

As for the South's mega-markets—there were seven with two million or more in population at the beginning of the twenty-first century: Baltimore-Washington-Northern Virginia, Houston, Dallas-Fort Worth, St. Louis, Atlanta, Tampa Bay, and South Florida—they have continued to diversify their population base as they have for the last 20 to 30 years. In the case of Baltimore and St. Louis, this diversity began more than 100 years ago.

Bombshell #7
The tide of public opinion, what I consider the 'final frontier,' has finally turned in the South's favor

While the sudden diversity of the South's population over the last 10 years has created new challenges, one byproduct of those challenges centers on the fact that the national media no longer "hammer" the South as they once did. Since the Civil War ended, the national media, once exclusively based in non-Southern locales, pounded the South every chance they could. I recall reading that a few years ago a popular California-based sports radio personality said on his show, "You folks are idiots down there. That's why no one lives down there" (the South). I guess he doesn't realize the South is home to 107 million people, a mere 44 million more than the number living in his region.

Let me give you some hard evidence of what I'm writing about. Take a look at the adjoining line art. This came from *The New York Times* right after Mercedes announced it was establishing its first North American assembly plant in Alabama. It is no wonder that such satirical cartoons were conspicuously absent when Honda (1999), Nissan (2000), and Hyundai (2002) announced they were investing billions in Mississippi and Alabama.

This bombshell is HUGE because instead of the South being perceived as outside the nation's mainstream, the tide of public opinion has changed. The national media are increasingly portraying the South as mainstream. I firmly believe that perception IS reality and if you subscribe to this belief too, you'll agree that the media's new presentation of the South is helping to drive the region's success.

Bombshell #8
The automotive industry has joined the party

Nothing has "primed the pump" quite like the automotive industry's incredible job and investment record in the South over the last 10 years. It accounts for hundreds of thousands of high-paying jobs in the region. To give you an example of how many jobs have been created by the expanding Southern automotive industry, all you have to do is go back to the late 1970s. Back then, Tennessee was home to around 20 automotive suppliers. Today, over 900 automotive suppliers are operating in the Volunteer State.

Part of what has attracted this huge supplier base to Tennessee is the presence of a major manufacturer. In 1983, Nissan selected Smyrna for its first U.S. vehicle assembly plant to build several of its top-selling models and employ 5,400 people. The company went on to announce a second Tennessee facility in Decherd in 1997 with a subsequent expansion in 2000.

Maybe you've heard South Carolina's story. BMW chose the Palmetto State for its first North American assembly plant in 1992. That facility has since expanded several times. Mississippi garnered Nissan two years ago and has announced an expansion of the plant prior to its opening. Kentucky has also been very proficient in attracting automotive facilities, as has virtually every other state in the South. Several Southern states now rank among the highest in the U.S. in terms of automotive production.

And then there's Alabama. No state in the American South has seen its auto industry grow and expand like Alabama's has over the last 10 years. While Tennessee, Kentucky, and North Carolina currently have more suppliers, Mercedes and Honda are in the middle of massive expansions and Hyundai is just beginning to construct its newest North American plant here. There is no doubt in my mind that automotive suppliers will be flocking to Alabama in the next few years and don't forget that Toyota has just established a large engine plant in Huntsville.

Bombshell #9
The South leads all other U.S. regions in foreign direct investment

Foreign investment, particularly from Japan and Western Europe, continues to pour into the South faster than any other region in America. Each year since the early 1990s, the total foreign investment gap has widened between the South and the three other U.S. regions. Today, the South is home to 40 percent of the dollars invested by foreign companies in the U.S. (1999 figures). Yes, that's a full 40 percent today—especially impressive when you consider that the South is comprised of only 17 of the 50 states. In 1992, the foreign investment in the South represented 35 percent of the nation's total.

Why is being the No. 1 region for foreign investment in the No. 1 economy in the world such an accomplishment? Foreign companies can choose any location in the U.S. in which to invest their time, resources, and energies. While that's sometimes the case with domestic companies, many are tied to their locations for a variety of reasons. So, if the majority of foreign companies are opting for one region over another year after year, it is proof of that region's ever-growing attractiveness.

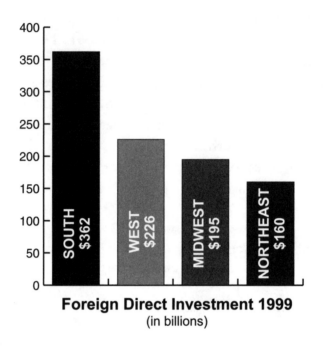

Foreign Direct Investment 1999
(in billions)

Source: U.S. Statistical Abstract 1999

Bombshell #10
The South is THE MAJOR political force

Politically, the South possesses great influence. As of 2002, the third Southerner in a row occupies the Oval Office. In fact, you have to go back to 1980 to find a non-Southern President being elected.

This influence isn't limited to the Presidency. Southerners by and large have been running the federal government as of the beginning of the twenty-first century. From the Senate Majority Leader to Speaker of the House, Southerners hold major positions of influence.

Another interesting point is that the region has virtually abandoned the Democratic Party, to which it was once almost completely loyal. The South is now reshaping American politics and propelling the GOP (the party of Abraham Lincoln, the Union, and Reconstruction!) into the majority. The white South today is becoming more and more Republican—the party of conservatism—in its politics, and it is Southerners who seem to be the **most** conservative members of the Republican Party. Indeed, it is Southern Republicans who have led the attack on the welfare state.

Electoral votes are another big story. As of 2000, the South held 195 of the total 270 votes needed to elect a President. Presidential candidates must woo the South if they want to be successful.

If the last 50 years are any indication of what the South can do, watch out!

All in all, the South has entered the twenty-first century remarkably strong. Just as the mythical Phoenix arose from the ashes, the South has risen from its challenging past more confident than ever with a long and growing list of advantages for companies and families alike.

As a recent article in *The Economist* magazine explains, "The mood is different in the South . . . Few Southerners worry as many Northerners do about whether they can afford the houses, college education and other luxuries of their fathers. Instead they are on an economic roll; such a strong one indeed, that they are pulling the rest of the country with them."

Even after coming so far so fast, the South's momentum is still powerful and it continues to build. That's the Southern way! We master momentum to embrace change. Southerners have transitioned from reacting to the outside forces of change imposed upon them, to becoming agents of change for the future.

If you are a corporate leader or business owner looking for a low-cost, pro-business location with a culture that will back your success 100 percent, read on. We'll detail the South's incredible attributes for profitable business operations.

If you are an individual climbing the corporate ladder, it is vital to determine where that ladder can best be leaned. We'll examine how living in the South can positively impact your career and the quality of your family's life.

To fully appreciate the South's economic momentum and potential, we'll start with an understanding of the past. We'll examine how the region has gone from poverty to prosperity in 50 years and where we'll go from here. But first, we'll define the "South."

two

Down Home

So Where Exactly Is the "South?"

Southerners can laugh at themselves—a rare quality. Sure, you've heard the jokes: "You know you're in the South when you hear someone use the pickup line 'nice tooth.' "

"You know you're a Southerner when after a hailstorm, you have to pull your home to the local body shop to have it repaired."

Or how about, "You know it's the South when you can order boiled possum with biscuits at the local McDonald's."

Better yet, "You know it's the South when the average belt buckle weighs more than a small child."

For a long time now America has had a good chuckle at the South's expense. Referring to Southerners as rednecks; accusing them of lacking sophistication. Behind all that good-natured ribbing, however, the South's keenly independent spirit has helped it become what it is today. It has helped enable and inspire the South to achieve a special character that sets it apart from all other regions.

From bubbas, pickup trucks, and manners . . . to "yes ma'am," hound dogs, and grits; it is truly a one-of-a-kind place. As great Southern historian W.J. Cash described in his book *The Mind of the South,* the region is "not exactly a nation within a nation, but the next thing to it."

So, if the mere mention of the South can conjure up such clear mental images why is it so hard to define in terms of the states that comprise it?

One often-used border is the Mason-Dixon Line, the boundary between Pennsylvania and Maryland that set the Northern limit for slavery. The greater part of this line has existed since 1767, when Charles Mason and Jeremiah Dixon, English astronomers who had been appointed to settle a dispute between the colonies, surveyed it. Although it is one of the oldest ways to define the region, the "south of the Mason-Dixon line" area includes states that simply are not Southern to most people, such as Maryland and Delaware as well as the Washington D.C. area.

Mason-Dixon Line

Occasionally, the Ohio River is considered another boundary for the South. This definition puts Kentucky in the South, even though in 1861 it fought for its native son Abraham Lincoln (not of Illinois as commonly thought) against another native son, Jefferson Davis.

Ohio River

Many purists see the "South" as the old Confederacy, the 11 states that seceded from the Union in 1860. This consists of Virginia, North Carolina, South Carolina, Georgia, Florida,

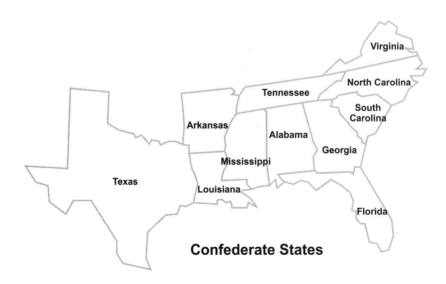

Confederate States

Tennessee, Alabama, Mississippi, Louisiana, Arkansas, and Texas.

Over time the South has naturally defined itself as a Right-to-Work region. "Right-to-Work" refers to the idea that workers cannot be required to join a labor union to keep their jobs. What these states have in common is high worker productivity and low union affiliation. Southerners by their very nature tend to be honest and hardworking persons, standing on their rights to choose who they run with. The very thought of being forced to do something or join a particular group just because someone else says to is not acceptable. Southerners typify the terms "choice" and "loyalty."

**Southern
Right–to–Work States**

Yet another definition comes from the U.S. Census Bureau. Interestingly, Census Bureau parameters include Delaware and Puerto Rico, but not Kansas.

**US Census
Bureau South**

Last, but certainly not least, is the Southern Economic Development Council (SEDC's) South. SEDC is the region's premier professional and political group of men and women who are promoting economic growth in the region. Its member-states total 17, which span from Texas to Maryland.

SEDC States

Since our primary focus is the South's tremendous economic boom, we'll define our "South" by SEDC's member-states. All of the comparisons in this book will be based on using the SEDC member-states vs. the nation (unless otherwise indicated).

Another reason I've chosen to go with SEDC's map is because leaders in these states have freely chosen to align themselves with the South. These states are all economically bound to the South on a voluntary basis, rather than by a government drawing bureaucratic lines.

Among SEDC's members, not all of the states are equally Southern. South Florida, for instance, more closely resembles Latin America (and provides the perfect gateway for companies wanting to do business in Central and South American markets). Kansas, Maryland, and Missouri also lack some of the "feel" of the South. Most of Texas feels more like the west—snakeskin boots, cactus, cowboys, and all. Regardless, every one of these states proudly calls itself "Southern" and belongs to SEDC.

Sociologist John Reed agrees. He is more interested in culture than geography and has studied this issue for years using survey data. He puts it simply that some areas of the South are more Southern than others. Historian James Cobb concurs; he has argued that the Yazoo-Mississippi delta is *The Most Southern Place on Earth*. While each of the South's different sub-regions has its own unique culture, Reed believes based on his research that a large number of unique cultural characteristics persist in the region, distinguishing it from other areas of the country.

This leads me to another interesting point. The more I've tried to define the South, the more I'm convinced that the South is much more than geography. I believe that the South is best defined not by borders but by "a peaceful state of mind."

It can also be defined by attitudes, starting with family. By this I mean both the predominance of family values and the importance placed on family. More than anywhere else in America, family is serious business in the South. A fascination with heritage is not only found among the "well to do." Regular folks here are more likely to know their family tree, get acquainted with their cousins, or care for their elders. Other common denominators of the South include such things as good manners, "funny" accents, and a love of sports.

A sense of family-oriented loyalty also emerges in the strong work ethic that defines the South. Sunup-to-sundown dedication, longevity, and the lack of an entitlement mentality are characteristic of the Southern worker. Team players are the norm rather than the exception. And once forged, loyalty remains.

Religion is another defining force, although the trend of rising diversity seems to be eroding this influence. Most Southerners are Protestant and the lines between church and state are often blurred. Roads are named after church leaders, such as Billy Graham Parkway in Charlotte.

In his work, *The South for New Southerners*, the University of North Carolina's John Shelton Reed has come up with some other interesting definitions for the South. One, whether or not a place is mentioned in country music songs; another is the sheer numbers of Baptist churches. And then there is Kudzu, an incredibly invasive vine that even though it is not a native thrives in the majority of the South. It does not discriminate, overtaking trees, cars, and even houses if given the opportunity. Other defining factors include an amazing diversity of cuisine, lack of frozen precipitation, and hospitality that extends to service and cooperation.

Perhaps most importantly, the South can be defined as the area where people call themselves "Southerners." The more militant among these have gone as far as pushing for "ethnic group" status. A true Southerner works hard to be his "own man" or "own woman" and takes pleasure in devising ways to be unique. Their colorful history, shared culture, and definite pride are communicated in how these individuals live and work. Southerners also share optimism, as more of them than ever before are living the American dream.

In the last generation, Southerners have learned that sustaining the "Southern way" doesn't require them to stay in poverty. The resilient Southern culture is being adapted to technology, wealth, and mobility. As the sociologist Reed pointed out, the Southern subculture seems to be remarkably adaptive to these incursions and resistant to elimination.

"So is there any reason, anymore, to talk about the South as 'the South?'" Reed questions. "Well of course there is. The South has always been as much a cultural region as an economic one. From the start, the South has been the home of people whose intertwined cultures have set them off from other Americans. And where the economic and political story has been largely one of conflict, division and separation, the tale of the cultural South is one of blending, sharing, mutual influence and continued distinctiveness."

As a 1994 article in *The Economist* magazine explains, "It is hard to visit the South even for a short time and come away with the feeling that it is just another part of America. The burden of history is too great; Southern hospitality too all-embracing; even the drawling accent too different." Conformity will not envelop the culture of the South.

Ultimately, the very best way to define the South in my opinion is by the "Hell, yes!" line, a term coined by North Carolina state senator Hamilton Horton . . . You know you're in the South if that's what people say when you ask them if they're Southerners!

three

Where We Came From

The Pre-World War II South

The South was America's "number one economic problem." That is how President Franklin D. Roosevelt described the region in 1938. Poverty, illiteracy, out-migration and infant mortality rates were outrageously high. A scarcity of capital and racial problems were also the harsh reality. Profound devastation from the Civil War still lingered.

The South's story didn't begin this way at all. Before 1860, the region was lavishly wealthy, standing just behind Britain and its Northern United States counterpart in per-capita income. But in its struggle to become its own nation, it was defeated.

Five years of Civil War did serious damage to the region. Railroads were destroyed; shipping terminals disrupted; equipment confiscated and most of what remained of the scant industry lay in disrepair and disarray. Confederate currency and bonds were worthless. Cotton surpluses in warehouses had been confiscated by Union troops. Farms and fields were in dire need of repair and critical machinery and equipment had been stolen. Plus the slave-labor supply totally eliminated.

Unlike the North, virtually all of the South's land, cities, and railroads were impacted by the war. Led by General William T. Sherman, Northern forces burned entire communities, wrapped railroad tracks around trees, and destroyed crops. The recovery effort was to be long and painstaking.

Why was the South so slow to emerge after the Civil War? Some theorists point to the out-and-out devastation . . . to the great loss of human life, livestock, and physical destruction. But in reality, Southern railroads were reconstructed by 1867 and Southern manufacturing (what little existed) was rebuilt by 1870.

Others point to the decline in agricultural output. This decline was partly caused by a fall in the per-acre output of cotton (driven by price drops) along with the drop in labor availability after the emancipation of slaves.

Still another problem was racial segregation, detailed by Gunnar Myrdal in *An American Dilemma*, published a few years after Roosevelt's remark. According to *The Economist's* 1994 Survey of the American South, "The urge to preserve segregation made white Southerners highly resistant to change."

Whatever the reasons, the South struggled for nearly a century after the Civil War to rebuild itself and to achieve economic equality with the nation as a whole. By contrast, other countries ravaged by war (such as Germany and Japan) were able to rebuild their economies within a decade with the help of massive amounts of foreign aid. The South's economic weaknesses significantly pre-dated the War Between the States and in reality, could be traced back to colonial days.

Early in American history, Southerners discovered the profitability of crops such as tobacco, indigo, and rice. To successfully grow these crops, they needed plenty of land and water, which were readily available in the region. They also needed cheap labor. Out of this need for workers, slavery became a reality of the American South.

By the 1830s, New Orleans had surpassed New York as America's busiest seaport. On the surface, the South was riding high. But underneath loomed inherent weaknesses in the Southern economy, which would spell disaster.

For example, the predominance of the self-sufficient plantation meant that urban centers were not necessary. The South had very few large cities that could mature into hubs of economic activity.

This also lessened the need for a transportation network such as roads and railroads. The region had very few deepwater ports, limited railroads, and little capital to build any substantial infrastructure. This lack of an integrated transportation network meant rural isolation for a high percentage of the population.

Capital was concentrated in the purchasing of slaves, leaving little or no cash for other development. In many areas of the South, the economy was 100 percent built on slavery. Therefore, Southerners had little need to pursue manufacturing investment. Sadly, between 1860 and 1865, the South lost two-thirds of its total wealth.

And then there was "King Cotton." In the early 1800s, cotton was usually more than half of all of the total U.S. exports. Large fortunes were made from slavery and cotton. But the South's biggest mistake was to rely too heavily on this cash crop.

By 1860, the image of the Confederacy South's economy was still poor, but in fact the average per-capita income of $103 was good as far as the rest of the world was concerned (about the same as Switzerland) and was exceeded only by the North, Great

Britain, and Australia. And as the secessionist cries picked up in the slave states, it was South Carolina Senator James Hammond who proclaimed, "You dare not make war upon our cotton. No power on earth dares make war on it. Cotton is King." King Cotton.

Growing cotton on plantations had become so successful that it now dominated the South's economy. When the Civil War broke out over 60 percent of the total export value of goods shipped from the U.S. was cotton.

The pressure to grow a cash crop was so intense that it substantially displaced food production in the South. By the turn of the century, a significant portion of the rural South was malnourished. Diseases such as pellagra, hookworm, and malaria were common. The growing dependence on a single crop, cotton especially, kept the Southern economy from developing balance and more lucrative occupations. Malnourishment and grinding poverty were a sad irony in a region of fertile land, bountiful water supplies, and a temperate climate.

After the war, as more and more land worldwide began to grow cotton, the South suffered. Overproduction caused a significant drop in cotton prices. Cotton averaged approximately 15.1 cents per pound between 1870 and 1873. By 1898, it brought only an average of 5.8 cents per pound. Considering that it cost approximately 7 cents per pound for Southern farmers to produce the cotton, it's easy to see how fast the debt was growing.

The situation in the Post-Civil War South was bleak at best. Although Atlanta newspaperman Henry Grady coined the term "New South," Southerners continued to make the same economic mistakes. Cheap labor quickly replaced slavery as the South's commodity. Agriculture was sovereign, cities scarce, and infrastructure still remained virtually nonexistent. The South was stuck in economic backwardness, serving as "America's economic colony for cheap labor and raw materials."

In terms of population, no one was moving to the South. The U.S. immigrant boom bypassed the South completely, with people opting for the opportunities they found in the North. In the second major wave of immigration to the U.S., between 1865 and 1910, 25 million new immigrants arrived. Virtually none of these individuals chose any Southern state in which to start their new lives. In 1910, less than 2 percent of the South's population was born outside this region.

Along with population, per-capita income in the South was painfully low. Before 1860, more than half of the richest one percent of Americans resided in the South. As late as 1930, Dixie's per-capita income was roughly half of what it was elsewhere in the nation, and according to John Shelton Reed, director of the Institute for Research in Social Science and the Louis Harris Data Center at the University of North Carolina, rural poverty was even greater. The tremendous economic expansion between 1865 and 1914, which saw a tripling of per-capita real income, virtually bypassed the struggling South.

The region was also very reluctant to industrialize. Up to this point, the society had emphasized mobility. A planter could take all of his capital with him, which discouraged fixed investment. Merchants had no tradition of industrial innovation or of applying science-based technology to production processes. Landowners, who benefited from low wages and lack of mobility, held on dearly to the old system and had little incentive in investing in manufacturing, as confirmed in a report from The Gilder Lehrman Institute of American History.

Even when industry came south, it was slow to grow and relied on Northern investment. Northerners supplied the capital and controlled businesses in the South. For instance, even when the steel industry entered Birmingham, Ala., the North kept control to ensure that Birmingham never challenged Pittsburgh.

Predominantly, Southern industry was small-scale, local businesses. Another interesting fact is that industrial jobs were viewed as "for women" so that families could purchase what couldn't be grown on the farm. Investors developed small textile factories or one-room furniture factories.

Partly because of the lack of skilled, educated workers, the South also did not develop the fast-growing industry of the time. For instance, electrical equipment, chemicals, meat processing, and machine tool manufacturers would never even have considered a Southern location, according to Gilder Lehrman. Any industry that did develop was low value-added such as manufacturing rough textiles, turpentine, liquor, and tobacco products. Educated and experienced managers were also rare.

Clearly, the South lagged way behind the North in industrialization. By 1850, the slave states had about 42 percent of the nation's population, but only 18 percent of the manufacturing capacity. While the South was still fixated on agriculture, the North was investing in building its infrastructure and growing industries that would serve worldwide markets.

Differential freight rates also discouraged industry from taking root in the South. These rates meant that Southern industry paid more to ship goods by rail than did other parts of the nation. The highly industrialized Northeast enjoyed low railroad rates, partly because it was the most overbuilt area of the country. Since railroads were losing money in that region, owners tried to make it up in less competitive areas, such as the agricultural South, by charging more for rail service.

Lack of capital was also a major problem in the South, post-Civil War. Much of it had been consumed by the war effort or "relocated" to the North by heavy taxation. Precipitating this problem was the fact that the demand for manufactured goods was low, partly because Southern markets were so small. The Gilder Lehrman Institute also notes that the South had fewer entrepreneurs than other regions.

Aggravating the debt dilemma was the South's lien system. Historical researcher Philip Mullins explains that the South's lien system converted the Southern economy into a vast pawnshop. "The profit from this year's crop," he says, "was spent before the cotton was harvested. Next year's crop was spoken for before it was planted. Until the farmer paid off his debt completely, he was dependent upon his creditor merchant for every purpose. The creditor merchant usually forced his debtors to purchase supplies at non-negotiable, far inflated prices."

For this reason, most farmers in the South never paid off their debts. In 1892, for example, an exceptionally bad year for crops, many farms were foreclosed upon and sold, Mullins explains. It was due in no small part to the lien system that the roads that year were full of African-Americans begging for a place to live.

All of these weaknesses left the South utterly dependent on other parts of the nation for its very survival.

The South's banks were also in ruins. Banking laws set up after the Civil War also favored urban areas over rural and the rest of the nation over the South. According to C. Vann Woodard in *Origins of the New South*, the National Banking Act of 1863 favored cities over rural areas. By 1885, there was one bank per 16,600 people in the U.S., but only one to every 58,130 people in the (Confederacy) South (excluding Texas). In 1894, 123 counties in Georgia lacked state, national, or any other incorporated banks. In the few communities that had banks, the rules forbid them to lend money for real estate or farms. High interest rates kept farmers in debt and tended to perpetuate the South's heavy dependence on agriculture, Woodard explains.

During the war, the South had printed its own paper money and borrowed heavily. When it lost the war, its money was worthless and the region was mired in debt and disarray. Correspondingly, the federal government was extremely slow to grant charters to Southern banks.

While circumstances in the South were grim across the board, it was the African-American community in particular that struggled the hardest. Many were trapped in sharecropping, tenant farming, and debt. Long after the Civil War, they continued to be treated as inferior in terms of status, opportunity, and power. "Under the sharecropping system, blacks were little better off than slaves," *The Economist* says.

The fact that very few jobs were available in the South's small towns forced African-Americans to rely on white landowners. Sharecropping, which provided blacks with credit for tools, seeds, living quarters, and food in return for a portion of crops raised on land they did not own, became the standard. This system was backed by "black codes," which limited African-Americans' ability to leave rural areas and reduced educational opportunities. Even when they did own land, blacks struggled with poor access to credit and a growing anti-black sentiment in the South.

Within two decades of the end of the Civil War, most Southern states had passed laws requiring racial separation. The "Jim Crow" laws mandated two sets of schools, two sets of restaurants, restrooms, park benches, and drinking fountains in every

Southern town. Separate housing areas developed and blacks were banned from pursuing many professional occupations.

Equally discouraging to African-Americans, disfranchising laws were passed in several Southern states. These discriminatory measures mandated that voters pass a literacy test and pay a poll tax before they could vote. The laws were in effect set up to discourage blacks from voting. This segregationist practice would hold back the South until the 1970s when the inevitable repercussions would begin to take hold of the nation as well as the South.

In the years immediately following the Civil War, most African-Americans remained in the South. Somewhere around 90 percent of all U.S. African-Americans lived in the region until as late as 1910. From 1910-1920, however, the out-migration of blacks from the South skyrocketed. These men and women were driven out of the region by hostility, lack of opportunity, and appalling economic conditions. Also, during World War I, Northern industries worked hard to attract blacks to greener economic pastures—a strategy that proved effective.

African-American population distribution and migration patterns can be traced using maps published in statistical atlases prepared by the U.S. Census Bureau for each Census from 1870 through 1920. By 1890, Census maps begin to show emerging concentrations in many of the North's urban areas such as New York City, Philadelphia, Pittsburgh, Cleveland, Toledo, and Chicago.

For example, the African-American population in Chicago was exploding and although the North was no promised land, conditions were better for African-Americans there than where they had been. Most migrants who left almost never returned.

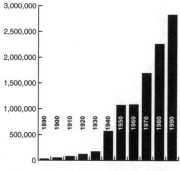

African-American Population in West
1890-1990 (U.S. Census Bureau Regions)

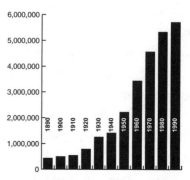

African-American Population in Midwest
1890-1990 (U.S. Census Bureau Regions)

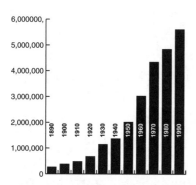

African-American Population in Northeast
1890-1990 (U.S. Census Bureau Regions)

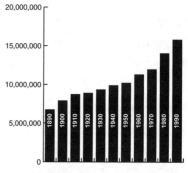

African-American Population in South
1890-1990 (U.S. Census Bureau Regions)

Population of Chicago by Decades—1830-2000

The following table shows the population of Chicago between
1830 and 2000. During the large periods of greatest growth,
many of the new residents of Chicago were African-Americans
fleeing the South.

1830 figures are approximated. The figures for 1840 to 2000
are from the U.S. Census of Population taken every ten years.

What made this out-migration of African-Americans from
the South particularly devastating was the fact that the blacks

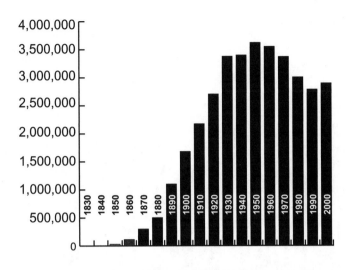

Population of Chicago by Decades
1830-2000

Compiled by Chicago Municipal Reference Library
Updated by Municipal Reference Collection, Chicago Public Library

leaving were in the prime of their working lives. Most of them were between the ages of 18 and 35 (in their most economically productive years). And because of racial limitations on certain professions, the African-Americans leaving the South were among the better educated.

By the late 1800s and early 1900s, the Southern economy slowly began shifting away from farming and toward manufacturing. Many African-Americans in Southern states were pushed out of skilled manufacturing jobs to make room for whites. While many paper mills were built in the South in the early 1900s, most were reluctant to employ African-Americans. The chart below shows a few of the Southern states and the drop in number of African-Americans who held skilled manufacturing jobs during 1910 (dark notation bar) and then in 1920.

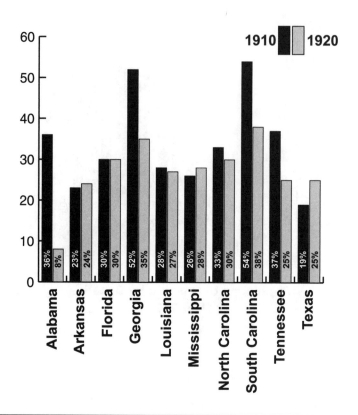

60

50

40

30

20

10

0

1910 ■ □ 1920

	1910	1920
Alabama	36%	8%
Arkansas	23%	24%
Florida	30%	30%
Georgia	52%	35%
Louisiana	28%	27%
Mississippi	26%	28%
North Carolina	33%	30%
South Carolina	54%	38%
Tennessee	37%	25%
Texas	19%	25%

(Source: Harrison, Alferdteen, eds., *Black Exodus: the Great Migration from the American South*. Jackson: University Press of Mississippi, 1991.)

Another lingering effect from the Civil War was the fact that the South was determined to remain independent. Most of the South's population, along with its leadership, continued to act as if it was a separate country. As we look back now, it seems that the South simply could not comprehend a new direction and thus sadly, it remained tethered to its past. It was reluctant to emulate or deal with its Northern neighbor. It was not until the 1930s that the South finally began to break free from this self-imposed isolation.

As early as the late 1800s, a few visionaries saw the "writing on the wall" for the South. Southerners such as Henry Grady, editor of the *Atlanta Constitution*, began urging the region to industrialize. According to John Beck, Wendy Frandsen, and Aaron Randall in *Southern Culture*, the arguments for industrialization were purely practical: industry had helped the North win the Civil War and industry was making the North rich. Further, the limits of the cotton economy in the South and of agriculture in general were becoming painfully obvious as the nineteenth century waned. What we need, Grady and others said, is a "New South," a South of industries and cities. What was also needed was a new Southern worker who, unlike his hard-working agrarian predecessors, was also hard-driving, competitive, and eager to make a buck.

Sadly, even by 1930, the South's economy had changed very little since 1870. It was still predominantly agricultural and rural. The region produced raw materials for export and was capital deficient. Sharecropping, tenant farming, and a crop-lien system kept many Southerners trapped in debt without economic opportunity. The limited industry that existed in the region was primarily low-wage. Dixie lacked urban centers, with only a few railroad towns, one-industry towns (usually textiles), and county seats dotting the landscape.

Across the South land ownership was still concentrated in a few hands, a legacy of the region's plantation past. And agriculture, the historic basis for the region's economy, still employed more than a third of the workforce in the 1940s. Unfortunately, it was still tied for the most part to a single crop . . . cotton.

A 1938 Report on the Economic Conditions of the South identified *"economic colonialism"* as the underlying reason. The report also blamed absentee ownership of Southern industry, and rail and river transportation for draining away the region's profits.

Worse still, as Lumpkin notes in *The South in Progress*, all these obstacles sharply restricted the promise for future improvement. A 1940 study put it this way: *"The effect is to keep the South poor, and to put the people at the mercy of an impersonal outside economic power."*

But within the next few years, starting in the late 1930s and early 1940s, the South began to recognize a profound need for change. It stood at the brink of an economic revolution.

four

The Tide Starts
to Turn

The Post-World War II South

With the seeds of destiny sown, the South changed virtually overnight!

By the end of World War II, the South had begun its agrarian-to-industrial revolution. Southerners had awakened to the reality that they had no choice—their economy HAD to change. The challenges of the past behind them now, Southerners were prepared to work harder and smarter to attract industry. These men and women were willing to do whatever it took to get results. Their motivation was high; their spirits resilient; and their memories long.

As a result, the industrial growth rate in the South increased exponentially. State governments actively courted Northern industry, extolling the virtues of the region's climate, large labor supply, its "competitive" (also known as "low") wage rates, and its favorable labor climate (meaning unions weren't exactly welcomed). Soon, state governments across the South softened their regulations to be more pro-business. They began offering inducements, "incentives" as they were referred to, ranging from subsidized workforce training and infrastructure to lower taxes. Modern industrial recruitment was invented in and by the South!

The Southern states were aggressive, determined, and most importantly, successful. As Bob Goforth, a Southern economic developer with more than 50 years of experience, remembers, "In the early days (1940s and 1950s), industrial developers literally raised money on the streets to finance locating industry. They worked hard to get one company settled and then would go after another one. Their success gave them the incentive to go after more companies."

Goforth's personal experience illustrates the South's intense pursuit of industry: "Industry hunters from the South would go to the garment district of New York in two-man teams to knock on doors," he recounts. "On one of these trips, my partner and I were sitting in the lobby of a sewing operation waiting to see the CEO. A young man came out and said 'I work here, but I'd like to have my own company. A friend told me that he would contract me to sew 6,000 dozen ladies' blouses (a fact we verified). We returned to North Carolina and chose a small town in a rural area to locate this man's operation. We went to the President of the local family-owned bank and asked him to lend the money to build a 20,000-square-foot building, which we gave to the new company with the first three months rent-free. Then, we personally rented used sewing machines for the operation. We got our state-funded training program cranked up and trained a labor force. With our hard work, the company grew and prospered in the South."

Industry began to trickle in, which was real progress for the South. The floodgates would open later.

The Great Depression, the New Deal, and World War II were three historic events that deeply affected the South's evolution over the 1950s, according to Numan Bartley in *The New South 1945-1980*. As late as 1938, two-thirds of the South's population lived in communities of less than 2,500. But over two decades (the 30s and 40s), the three following events helped reinvent the South.

The Great Depression hit the South especially hard. Desperate communities went after new industry at virtually any cost. Grants and concessions were presented without concern for legality, and many times in defiance of it. In Tennessee, for example, smaller industry-hungry communities forced workers to buy their new jobs by docking paychecks five to seven percent to pay for a company's new factory.

The New Deal helped short-term. It brought in capital in the form of federal projects, which created jobs. But it also helped in the long term. It raised the general population's awareness of economic issues. In the 1960s, it also influenced pragmatic Southern politicians like Lyndon Johnson to pursue federally financed programs and projects. Many of the New Deal projects were commissioned by the Works Progress Administration (WPA). By 1943, WPA had put some $11 billion into building or improving more than 2,500 hospitals, 5,900 school buildings, and nearly 13,000 playgrounds.

The Tennessee Valley Authority was another innovative New Deal creation. Prior to its creation, massive flooding and devastation were commonplace in the Tennessee Valley area (which includes parts of Alabama, Mississippi, Kentucky, Georgia, North Carolina, and all of Tennessee). Then, during the 1940s, TVA carried out THE largest hydropower construction program in U.S. history. At its peak (in 1942) projects at 12 locations were in progress at the same time. The design and building work employed 28,000 people. Within three years, the TVA became the nation's largest electricity supplier and brought affordable electric power to rural residents, making their lives easier and more productive. But more importantly, it also became a significant contributor to the economic development of several Southern states.

Still, even with Roosevelt's New Deal initiatives, the South remained a "low-wage region in a high-wage country," according to economist Gavin Wright. Ironically it was in the "buckle" of the Deep South's Cotton Belt where a major turning point in the South's economy took place.

With a single, brilliant decision, Mississippi lit the fire of economic growth. It became the first state in the nation to offer incentives to locating industry.

In *The Selling of the South*, James Cobb notes that manufacturing per capita in the other Southern states was four times higher than in Mississippi when Governor Hugh White won legislative approval in 1936 for a "Balancing Agriculture with Industry" (BAWI) program. BAWI was the first formal, state-sanctioned program to subsidize industry. Essentially, it allowed Mississippi to sell bonds in world financial markets to bring capital into the state. Then, Mississippi could offer that money to companies willing to bring jobs.

BAWI began with a $100,000 budget to "publicize the agricultural and industrial possibilities" of Mississippi. Somehow it didn't seem to matter that the state's constitution specifically prohibited use of public revenue to aid private individuals, firms, or corporations. By introducing an industrial recruitment program based on state-sanctioned and supervised use of municipal bonds to finance plant construction, Cobb notes, BAWI lifted the curtain on an era of competitive incentives. It also quickly expanded state and local government's involvement in industrial development.

BAWI heightened competition among the Southern states for new industry. The use of municipal industrial development bonds spread rapidly across the South. Industrial bond issues in Tennessee alone (all illegal according to the state's constitution) involved nearly three times as much money as those in Mississippi.

With the advent of incentives, industry could be even more selective in its determination of where to locate. The focus of site searches narrowed to only those locations that could meet critical requirements such as labor, markets, or materials. Once these sites were identified, the company could then bargain among the competing communities for the best financial package.

In response, states and communities searching for the "edge" needed to steal industries away from competing locations. This process reinvigorated the use of tax exemptions and it inspired the formation of development agencies dedicated to providing manufacturers with the capital necessary to build factories and start production.

In most cases these development agencies grew from New Deal state planning commissions, according to Bartley. They advertised the virtues of their states. In addition, they provided assistance for companies establishing new plants or expanding old ones. In varying degrees, they also helped train workers, provided low-cost or free land, constructed plants, and reduced a corporation's taxes.

State governments were the first to get into the game, led by Mississippi and North Carolina. Counties, cities, and municipalities quickly followed. Even rural areas pursued economic growth with Tupelo, Mississippi, of all places leading the way in 1948.

At that time, Tupelo was located in the poorest area in America. Then, newspaper owner George McLean established the Community Development Foundation (CDF), which successfully lured furniture makers and other small manufacturers. "Instead of relying on grants and tax breaks," The Economist explains, "it prepared industrial sites and workers."

As long-time CDF President Harry Martin recalls, all adults employed in manufacturing were required to undergo retraining every five years. Even today, the city's vocational program is impressive, admired, and emulated regularly.

As these development groups evolved, so did the profession of "industry hunting." Industrial developers became experts in "target" industries such as cut and sew, chemicals, or textile production. By specializing, they were able to "speak the language" of a particular industry, know the needs and requirements for a new location, and, ultimately, become more effective at selling the South.

Still, as Morton Sosna observed in *Perspectives on the American South*, it was World War II that had "a greater impact than the Civil War" on the economy of the South.

During the years of World War II, factory construction and expansion doubled the South's industrial plant level from 1939, note historians such as Hoover and Ratchford, Wright, and Polenberg. Manufacturing capacity also significantly increased and correspondingly industrial employment jumped from 1.6 million workers to a high in late 1943 of 2.8 million, according to Bartley. While pay scales in the South remained below national averages, the requirements of the Fair Labor Standards Act of

1938 and the policies of the War Labor Board during the war years forced Southern wages upward.

Shipbuilding and plane fabrication yielded an industrial bonanza. Shipbuilding in Pascagoula, Mississippi, vaulted the population from 4,000 in 1940 to 30,000 in 1944. Naval production moved Mobile's metropolitan population from 115,000 in 1940 to 200,000 in 1944.

In Dallas-Fort Worth and Atlanta-Marietta, giant aircraft factories fueled further urban growth. Ordinance plants appeared throughout the region—the making of ammunition and explosives became the most geographically scattered of the South's wartime industries. Coal production expanded in the Upper South. Petroleum and chemical industries grew enormously in the Southwest. This was especially true in Texas—the Southern state that experienced the largest economic gain from wartime spending.

Even more money—about $4.75 billion—went into military installations, related housing, and other public projects as the South became the training ground for the nation's armed forces, Bartley adds.

Also during World War II, the South's economy benefited from the government's dispersion policy. This policy directed industry to locate where it would be (in theory) out of harm's way. The rural South was ideal for this purpose, according to Goforth.

The dispersion policy also helped Northern industry recognize the standout qualities of the South's workforce. Goforth indicates that once industries discovered the region; they were pleasantly surprised as well as extremely pleased by what they encountered. The workforce had been primarily raised on farms and possessed a tremendous work ethic. Additionally they had strong family ties and showed great loyalty to those who treated them fairly.

By 1944 government payrolls accounted for some 25 percent of salaries and wages in the region. This helped create markets for small businesses and jobs for numbers of people. In all, from 1940-1945, about one quarter of the region's farm population—a figure totaling four million—was now working in industry. No longer was the South heavily agrarian. Its postwar economy had radically changed.

The federal government remained a major employer. A study of the 1952 Census showed that the South received $1.50 in federal funds for every dollar it paid in taxes. Another study estimated that in 1955 one of every ten dollars of personal income in the region was wages and salaries the federal government directly disbursed to military and civilian employees. Even so, a study by Wright cited in Fred McMahon's *The Road to Growth* found that per-capita federal capital expenditures in the South in 1952 were only 83 percent of the national average and from 1959-1961 these expenditures had only increased by 5 percent.

The fifties were also a time when the cost of living was rising. Farming had become less and less profitable, but the wartime dispersion policy and the rise of bond financing (and other subsidies) across the South had produced a heavy concentration of competitive, wage-sensitive industries like textiles. In these businesses, stiff competition and slim profit margins required savings in wages, fringe benefits, and spending on new plants.

The South's lower cost structure was its number one attraction, post-World War II. Companies, however, were also recognizing that the South was a developing market for their products, full of people who wanted to work as well as purchase the latest goods for their families.

As a result, cheap, nonunion labor remained a key element in the South's appeal to new industry. Promotional ads of the immediate postwar period capitalized on this. The South Carolina Planning Board, for example, assured investors that the average laborer in the Palmetto State "has never heard of one loom to a weaver in cotton mills."

The reason why: organized labor in Dixie dated back only as far as the New Deal. Unions had surfaced as a byproduct of FDR's National Industrial Recovery Act. But, union membership grew only half as fast in the South as it did in the rest of the nation from 1939-1953. No major gains for organized labor below the Mason-Dixon Line occurred in the fifties.

And no wonder. Southern politicians were some of the loudest supporters of the 1947 Taft-Hartley Act. This law rewarded companies for resisting unions. More importantly, it encouraged Southern legislatures to pass Right-to-Work laws, which prevented workers from being forced to join a union to get a job. And they ensured workers could not be forced to pay union dues if a workplace became unionized.

Arkansas and Florida led the Right-to-Work crusade with constitutional amendments in 1944. All the other Southern states except Kentucky and Oklahoma followed during 1947-1954 (Oklahoma has also joined the Right-to-Work bandwagon in recent years). As you might guess, the ever astute Southern development officials wasted no time in incorporating their Right-to-Work status into promotional advertising.

Labor leaders criticized the success of the bond programs in encouraging industrial migration to low-wage, nonunion areas, now mainly in the South. At its 1952 convention, the AFL condemned industrial bonds as both direct and indirect subsidies to industry. Organizers also criticized Southern resistance to unionization. They claimed it denied workers the full financial benefits of industrialization.

Unfortunately for the labor leaders, hard facts and numbers don't lie. From 1940-1950, average per-capita personal income rose 358 percent in the South. Meanwhile, the number of manufacturing plants locating there from 1939-1954 increased by 80 percent. Further intensifying the situation was a series of well-publicized plant relocations to below the Mason-Dixon Line. In record numbers, labor-troubled companies were replacing high costs and outdated plants with lower costs and streamlined facilities in the South. In 1954, for example, Textron operated 15 plants in the Northeast and nine in the South. But by 1957, the company had moved all of its plants to the South.

Since the interest on industrial bonds was exempt from federal tax, federal lawmakers began to voice their disapproval. In a series of speeches and articles Massachusetts Senator John F. Kennedy complained about Southern "raiding," particularly in the textile industry. In a 1954 *Atlantic Monthly* article, he questioned: "What happens when [the South's] newfound [industrial] benefactors leave for another bargain elsewhere?" Readers would have to wait 40 years for the answer.

Oddly, racism was also a part of Southern recruiters' promotional efforts. Capitalizing on a long-standing prejudice against recent immigrants and their affinity for labor unions, one advertisement lauding Louisville, Kentucky, pictured a worker with the caption "he speaks English!"

Such prejudice was mild compared to the South's rigid racism. Of all the region's identifying traits, its "Jim Crow" customs did not fit with its goal of becoming a modern industrial society. As national attention on civil rights issues mounted in the mid-fifties, most image-conscious, nationally known firms shied away from a region whose racial policies were so incredibly offensive to so many. As a result, most Southern industry hunters pushed for peaceful desegregation.

But while the Civil Rights Movement began to break down this major blemish on the South's image, the South had other big-time challenges to overcome for industrial progress.

From the mid-40s to the mid-50s, factories employing at least 25 workers had increased by one third, Bartley writes. These new plants produced a range of goods. Still, most were traditional low-wage, labor-intensive operations directly tied to agriculture. They made textiles, apparel, furniture, lumber, tobacco, and food products. Many engaged in the first-stage conversion of raw materials from Southern farms, forests, and mines. For this reason, they were located in and around towns where these materials were at hand and labor was cheap and abundant.

Even in the 50s, many of these communities still gave the physical appearance of backwardness and indifference. Public facilities were generally rundown or nonexistent. Throughout the decade, population numbers in the South's small towns stagnated.

A handful of the more prosperous towns became metropolitan areas. A range of sophisticated, capital-intensive, high-value-added "new industries" gravitated to these metropolitan areas to find skilled workers, transportation options, and services.

Economic developers now increasingly included real-estate dealers, construction companies, retailers, public utilities, bankers, and media executives as well as lawyers, doctors, and other professionals; all advocating reform. This diverse group of businesspersons wanted to enhance the South's appearance, moderate its racial tensions, and recruit more industry.

The skills that veterans had gained during their service in World War II were a big boost to the Southern workforce. At the same time, their access to the GI Bill and a college education also made them increasingly impatient with the lack of economic opportunity.

Governors McGrath of Arkansas and Browning of Tennessee were among the first to tackle industrial development with a new, businesslike approach to government. Rather than succumbing to the age-old patronage system of choosing cabinet members, these governors were committed to being accountable and to appointing people who could without a doubt get the job done. In Georgia, Governor Ellis G. Arnall single-handedly put an end to differential freight rates. He successfully argued before the Supreme Court that the higher inter-territorial (and intra-territorial) transportation charges Southern manufacturers of high-value finished goods had been forced to pay the railroads since the end of the Civil War were unfair.

Governor Arnall also noted that the rates on raw materials moving to the factories of the North from the South amounted to a subsidy to Northern manufacturers. He said this was especially true in parts of New England where obsolete plants might have required refitting without an effective subsidy.

His efforts led the Interstate Commerce Commission to equalize the rates (that dated back to the late 1860s) in 1952. Ironically, the following year, Dwight D. Eisenhower was elected President and began to push for a system of interstate highways that would have a profound effect upon the American economy. He modeled the highways after the German Autobahn which Hitler had used to successfully move vast quantities of military equipment. Appropriately, legislation to create the Interstate System was originally proposed by one of the South's favorite sons, Senator Albert Gore, Sr., of Tennessee.

Eisenhower and his staff worked for two years to get the world's largest public works project approved by Congress. On June 29, 1956, he signed the Federal Aid Highway Act. On August 2, Missouri became the first state to award a contract with the new interstate construction funding. By November, eight miles of new interstate highway had opened in Topeka, Kansas, as other states now pushed to get their own piece of the concrete pie.

In the mid-50s pro-business moderates held power in a number of Southern states. Leroy Collins of Florida and Luther Hodges of North Carolina were among the most outspoken. Both led administrations devoted to attracting new industry. But Hodges went so far as to call industrialization "the number one goal of my administration."

Collins created a "development credit corporation" to make loans to new enterprises, an industrial services division to tender assistance to new industries, and an international trade department to facilitate integration of goods and services to the world. He also set up a state advertising commission, a nuclear development commission, and had the Florida Development Commission coordinate the various state agencies devoted to attracting investors and tourists.

Hodges was even more inventive. He formed the first major state industrial development group and set it up along the lines of a private business. Some of his other innovations included having the governor participate in "sales" trips to promote the state, conducting overseas missions to attract foreign investment, and developing an industrial education center that ultimately evolved into a statewide community college system. Hodges also strengthened North Carolina's Department of Conservation and Development. And he lowered taxes on corporations.

He was unhappy that North Carolina's existing industry was mostly the traditional low-wage variety found across the South. The emergent, fast growing industries of the 60s and 70s would require more than well-trained workforces. Unfortunately, the South's research resources reflected its agrarian past. Southern universities were still much more likely to provide agricultural experimental facilities than anything helpful to industry. In the nation at large in 1948 there were 52 industrial researchers for every 10,000 wage earners, but in the South only 10. This led to Hodges' most innovative and successful economic development project—an ambitious program to attract technologically sophisticated and research-driven operations that he called the Research Triangle Park (RTP).

The points of the triangle—the University of North Carolina at Chapel Hill, Duke University at Durham, and North Carolina State University at Raleigh—surrounded a research triangle institute at its heart. Recognizing that tech-based companies lacked a place to locate in the South, Hodges modeled the park after similar areas around universities such as Stanford. He nursed the privately funded, state-supported research park through its difficult years. Then, by 1959, it became an established reality.

To accelerate its move toward the nation's economic mainstream, the South would have to provide a climate for invention, discovery, and innovation. That, my friends, is exactly what it would do.

five

The "Sunbelt" Rises

The 1960s

By the 1960s, the South's economy was changing before America's very eyes. The extent varied from state to state but the region as a whole was making major headway on most every socio-economic front. The majority of the population was transforming into metropolitan based communities and industry as well as commercial endeavors that overcame agricultural trending. Most Southerners worked in manufacturing, trade, or to a lesser degree, in services. The dire pronouncements of FDR's Report on the Economic Conditions of the South were quickly becoming a distant memory. A modern economy was its designated successor.

Air conditioning, first envisioned as an industrial tool and later as an enticement to get people to attend public entertainment, had swept suburban America in the 1950s. In Florida one in five homes had air conditioning by 1960, according to U.S. Census figures. In the South, air conditioning had also sparked dramatic changes. By the sixties, it had totally revolutionized the region's living and working environments by making the summer heat bearable.

The South's industrial recruitment focuses increasingly shifted to more sophisticated, better-paying industries. Many Southern industrial promoters joined the International Development Research Council. The world's most highly regarded association for economic development, this organization boasted more than 2,700 members in 44 international chapters. Increased professionalism led developers to survey deficiencies and identify obstacles. Not surprisingly, race relations and the quality of public education went on the hot seat.

"Upgrading Southern school systems hadn't been critical as long as low-wage, labor oriented industries had been the targets of choice," James Cobb writes in *The Selling of the South*. Industrialists always mentioned the importance of good schools in their site decisions yet when ranked against key criteria—highly productive, affordable labor and low taxes—the quality of education as well as schools quickly dropped off the radar screen.

In a survey of 105 corporate board chairmen, representatives from labor-intensive industries such as textiles and apparel admitted they did not examine local schools when selecting a new plant site. Predictably, firms that considered education most seriously were the technically oriented ones in fields like aerospace and electronics.

As a result of the new effort to attract higher-skilled jobs, per-pupil expenditures in the South—50 percent of the 1940 national average—were 78 percent of the national mean by 1968 in all but five states.

The desire for new industry had the greatest educational impact on vocational training. Attracting better-paying industries required the South to supply adequate numbers of well-trained workers. It needed to be as inexpensive for high-skill industries to move south as it already was for the lower paying, labor-intensive ones. Expanding vocational-technical programs was the best solution. Before the end of the decade, regional vocational-technical education centers within reasonable driving distance of every citizen in the South began to evolve. Tennessee, for example, spread 29 training facilities across the state from Memphis to Bristol.

To attract the kinds of new plants that would free its workforce from low wages, Cobb adds, South Carolina also pioneered a quick response worker-training program designed around a system of "special" schools. Its mission: to ensure new plants could open with a workforce that was "ready to go."

"You can start up in the black in South Carolina," promoters told prospects. The quick success of the South Carolina program spawned similar programs in other Southern states. Such state-financed training meant corporate cost savings. The Arkansas Industrial Development Commission estimated total savings for a medium-sized plant would be $91,000 per year in the 1960s.

The South's better-trained workers earned more than those already employed in textile and apparel plants. Even so, these skilled workers took home less money than their counterparts elsewhere in the nation, writes Cobb. Regardless, per-capita income in the South rose dramatically and increased more rapidly than it did nationally. In 1940 Southern incomes were 60 percent of the national average. By 1960 they had grown dramatically to 76 percent.

These rising incomes led to a better standard of living and more economic opportunity. People were eating better. They were living longer. They were consuming more than ever before. Not since the early years of the nineteenth century had Southerners enjoyed this kind of lifestyle.

With a steady influx of people from small communities and rural areas, the metropolitan areas boomed between 1940 and 1960. Metropolitan populations in the Census South swelled from 8 million to approximately 21 million people (43.5 percent of the region's total population). In short, the campaign to sell the South succeeded for the cities more than the towns. And the increased capital that came with the new residents fueled further metropolitan growth.

Texas and Florida were the fastest urbanizing of the Southern states. Each had populations that were approximately two-thirds metropolitan by 1960. In Florida, much of that growth came from the space program. Cape Canaveral, Florida, had been established as a long-range missile test site in 1949. It became the focus for the nation's aerospace efforts after NASA was created in 1958. Shortly after, it was transformed from scrubland into the launch base for Alan Shepard's 1961 space flight and to this day continues to attract the attention of the world.

On Shephard's safe recovery, President Kennedy announced that an American would land on the moon and return safely to Earth before the end of the decade. This led to the construction of a Mission Control Space Center in Houston. The Texas city was chosen from among 23 potential sites after it met all the essential criteria. These included availability of water transport, a first-class all-weather airport, and proximity to a major telecommunications network. Other criteria included the presence of prominent recognized universities, a well-established pool of industrial and contractor support, a readily available supply of water, a mild climate permitting year-round outdoor work, and a culturally attractive community. It did not hurt that the Vice President at that time was a Texan by the name of Lyndon Baines Johnson who coincidentally was also in charge of our space program.

Northern Alabama also benefited from America's space program. The Marshall Space Flight Center, established as a NASA field installation in 1960, provided the Mercury-Redstone vehicle that sent Shepard on his historic flight. It had also become home to the small group of German scientists rescued from Europe in 1945.

Back in Florida, NASA was authorized by Congress in 1962 to acquire more property. This property was eventually re-christened Cape Kennedy shortly after J.F. Kennedy's untimely death in 1963. NASA took title to 83,894 acres by outright purchase and negotiated for use of an additional 55,805 acres of state-owned (somewhat distressed as well as submerged) land with an investment that reached approximately $71 million.

In the same year, nine of the Southern states had already established industrial bonding programs, Cobb notes. Now almost any Southern community with adequate labor and services could be in the running for new industry.

Meanwhile, three urban areas—Houston, Dallas, and Atlanta—had reached populations of more than a million people each. A dozen more metro areas claimed more than a half million residents and were expanding rapidly.

Atlanta, Dallas, Memphis, and New Orleans were "branch-house" cities, Raper and Reid described. By this name, they acknowledged that executives employed by Northern-headquartered corporations dominated the business community in each. Most of the South's other major cities hosted "sub-regional headquarters" for national firms.

But of all the South's biggest cities in the 1960s, Atlanta and Dallas were unquestionably the two greatest regional metropolises, Bartley writes. Both had surged ahead of rival cities on the basis of wholesale and retail sales, business and service income, bank clearings, the number of corporate branch offices, and the value added by manufacturing. Both had established positions as commercial centers of the Southeast and Southwest respectively. And both were regional headquarters for the Federal Reserve Bank and transportation centers—first as railroad hubs, and later as connecting points for the new interstates and air travel.

The airports in these two mega-cities also ballooned. In 1961, Atlanta's airport (a small airfield with a dirt racetrack for a runway in 1925) opened a new jet age terminal designed for six million passengers per year of capacity. Even so, it was soon unable to accommodate demand as Atlanta vied for the distinction of becoming one of the world's busiest airports (it ranks number two as of 2002 behind Chicago's O'Hare). A master plan was initiated by 1966 to guide its future.

Dallas, engaged in an intense rivalry with nearby Fort Worth for the business of commercial aviation and carriers in 1964, began enlarging its Love Field airport. In response, Fort Worth was constructing Greater Southwest International Airport only 12 miles away. The Civil Aeronautics Board intervened. It required the two cities to arrive at a voluntary agreement to designate a single airport through which CAB-regulated carriers would service the area. Four years later, both entered into a contract providing for the construction and operation of a new Dallas-Fort Worth airport. It soon became one of the world's busiest airports (it ranks number three as of 2002, according to Airports Council International).

As centers of commerce, transportation, distribution, finance, insurance, and services, Atlanta and Dallas had much in common. But the two cities were also radically different.

Located strategically close to the Texas oil fields, Dallas performed administrative, financial, and service functions for the petroleum industry (an activity that declined as Houston gradually took over those roles and merged them into its own petrochemical domination). But more than most Southern metropolises, Dallas had become a manufacturing center and by the sixties specialized in light industry and the production of aircraft, oil machinery, and apparel.

Metropolitan Atlanta, which also had light industry and aircraft assembly plants, and both Ford and General Motors automobile assembly plants, had the added advantage of the headquarters of significant corporations—Coca-Cola, Georgia-Pacific, Delta Airlines—and numerous branch firms led by "overseer executives" from Northern backgrounds. Here, a black middle class emerged earlier than anywhere else in the country. Professional blacks—social workers, clerical workers, educators, and businesspeople—were growing in number. Also steadily increasing was the number of registered black voters, an issue at the heart of increasing racial tension in the South.

In Birmingham, a city of similar size to Atlanta in 1960, racial tension generated riots that drew negative national attention. The South's premier industrial city, Birmingham seemed to weave together the worst features of American industrialism, Northern absentee ownership, and Southern racism, according to Bartley.

But in Atlanta, as Fred McMahon writes in *The Road to Growth*, local officials and the business community were more open to integration than anywhere in the South. Atlanta advertised itself as the "city too busy to hate," and as a result enjoyed economic benefits that made it grow significantly faster than Birmingham.

Samuel Lubell had written in 1952 that "One of the most striking features of the economic revolution sweeping Dixie today is the degree to which the South has been able to transfer its traditional, agrarian rooted racial attitudes to the new emerging industrial society." As the nation became more and more outraged at the South's racism, an unexpected change in Southern politics would be required to cure this ill.

"For almost a century after reconstruction in the 1870s, Southern politics was one of America's great certainties," *The Economist Magazine* reported. "To white Southerners the Republican Party was the enemy. And so, the Democratic Party became an essential cornerstone of every white Southerner's life."

From 1880 to 1944 all 11 original Confederate states had voted by huge majorities for the Democratic Presidential candidate. All this changed with a civil rights bill President Truman proposed in 1947 to win black votes in the North. The political impact in the South was electric, with the Missouri-born Truman's perceived "duplicity" igniting a new "Dixiecrat" party for the 1948 Presidential race. South Carolina Senator Strom Thurmond was its candidate.

Democrats lost more ground in the 1960s, despite winning the decade's first two Presidential elections. And once again, a Southerner was at the center of the controversy.

Lyndon Baines Johnson was only the fourteenth Southerner to reach the nation's highest office when he became its 36th President. Led by Johnson, the Democratic Party believed that an activist government could end poverty in America, heal the nation's racial divisions, and improve the quality of life for everyone. Democrats enacted more social reform legislation in 1964 and 1965 than at any time since the New Deal.

Named by FDR in 1933 to head the National Youth Administration in Texas, Johnson had climbed the political ladder to Senate Majority Leader by 1954. A shrewd, skilled politician and consistent opponent of civil rights legislation, he developed strong personal relationships with conservative Southerners. Then in 1957, as part of his Presidential aspirations, he began supporting civil rights to appease liberal Democratic Party bosses.

Despite this, party leaders judged him too "sectional." The 1960 nomination went to Massachusetts Senator John F. Kennedy who selected Johnson as his running mate to "balance the ticket."

The momentum for civil rights grew during the Kennedy administration with three key events—the 1960 Sit-ins in Greensboro, North Carolina; the Freedom Rides of 1960; and the violent 1963 Birmingham protests. Eventually, the President was forced to send the Civil Rights Bill to Congress.

Kennedy's Civil Rights Bill was still in committee when his November 22, 1963 assassination in Dallas elevated Johnson to the White House. Here Johnson quickly proved a masterly, reassuring leader in domestic affairs. He guided a tax-reduction law through Congress—the Economic Opportunity Act—and in a far-reaching effort to reduce poverty and malnutrition, extend medical care, provide decent housing, and provide jobs for the impoverished, he launched his Great Society Program in 1964.

Having been instrumental in the passage of the 1957 Civil Rights Act, Johnson also took up passage of Kennedy's Civil Rights Bill as a monument to the fallen leader because "he believed in it," according to Robert MacNamara, who served under him. As a Southerner, Johnson recognized the political risk, commenting as he signed the bill into law, "I think I just lost the South."

He went on to win the 1964 Presidential election by a landslide. But his prediction about losing the South was not far off the mark—Republican challenger Barry Goldwater carried five

Deep South states. Even so, it was former Alabama Governor George Wallace who stole the nation's attention and focused it firmly on the South.

To many, Wallace embodied racism in America. Others saw him as a champion of Southern pride and a defender of the working class. After losing the 1958 Alabama gubernatorial election, Wallace easily won in 1962 after becoming the most defiantly pro-segregation candidate on the ticket. National exposure gained from his University of Alabama "schoolhouse door stand," subsequent civil rights marches, and violence in Alabama prompted him to enter a few of the 1964 Presidential primaries. His vigorous opposition to Johnson's Civil Rights bill resonated with many voters outside the South. As a result, the Wallace campaign easily outperformed the predictions before he dropped out of the race.

Running for the presidency again in 1968, Wallace carried most of the same Southern states Goldwater had in 1964. But unlike "Dixiecrat" Thurmond, Wallace did so by taking votes from Republicans rather than Democrats.

Johnson followed the 1964 Civil Rights Act with the Voting Rights Act of 1965, which MacNamara said, "he fought tooth and nail to get through." The Voting Rights Act was designed to eliminate barriers that had been used to restrict voting by black Southerners. Violence in Selma, Alabama, had highlighted the need for urgent action on the issue. Of 15,000 eligible Dallas County black voters in and around Selma, only 335 had been able to register. When nonviolent protesters descended on Selma to stage a march to the state capitol in Montgomery, Governor Wallace who two years earlier had promised "Segregation forever!" sent in state troopers in a futile effort to hold back time.

Many people in the South believed that order had been lost in society with the Passage of the Civil Rights and Voting Rights Acts—it proved totally the opposite. Through the racial struggle, the chains of bondage were removed not only from African-Americans, but from the Southern economy as well.

The emergence of black civil rights was one of the most significant events for the Southern economy. The economic benefits of integration for the South's companies included full access to the available labor force and reduced friction in the workplace.

As the tumultuous decade of the sixties closed, the South had surpassed the Northeast and Midwest in population. The immigrants to the South over the sixties, Bartley notes, were overwhelmingly white and often well educated. They moved mainly to Texas, Florida, and Virginia.

Meanwhile, the proportion of manufacturing jobs in the region had increased dramatically as this building bonanza became the forerunner of the high-rise office building boom. Hotels, restaurants, entertainment providers, convention centers, and athletic stadiums many times occupied land on which low-income black housing had once stood. Service-sector employees became essential. Finally, the South's economy had become more diversified.

six

The Migration Peaks

The 1970s

In the 1970s, the South moved into an era of incredible growth.

State governments were taking a more active role in pursuing industrial development. Growth was also driven by important social and political innovations that had swept through the South in the previous two decades.

The region's sales pitch to new industry became a curious blend of old, new, and the still to come. Familiar assurances of cheap nonunion labor, inexpensive land, and low taxes were given with promises of tailored workforces and research assistance provided at state expense. When these factors were coupled with the cry of "don't be last to take advantage," it provided a compelling message to industry.

By the 70s, North Carolina's Research Triangle had become in the words of historian James Cobb "the South's most successful high-technology venture."

Widespread mechanized farming had nearly eliminated the demand for cheap farm labor—the proportion of cotton picked by machine shot up from 10 percent in 1950 to 90 percent by 1970.

Small manufacturing had also taken off in the South—especially in states like Tennessee and Georgia. Low turnover, subsidized rent, tax breaks, worker training, and low-interest loans all contributed to this growth. The importance of smaller manufacturers to local economies went beyond providing jobs. They were also a key to providing component parts and products for the South's growing automotive, aerospace, and petrochemical sectors.

To Americans willing to forgive its often-held beliefs of "past transgressions," a resurrected South held out the prospect of easy, cheap living.

Florida was the cornerstone of this "new" South and as the space industry was continuing the boom experienced throughout the previous decade, Florida's population was now increasing by nearly 3,000 people per WEEK! These new Floridians had come in search of jobs, warm weather, and sunshine. By the early 1970s, they helped put the "Sunshine State" ahead of Virginia as the Southern state with the highest per-capita income.

Meanwhile, Florida remained the South's most dramatic tourist magnet. With long beaches facing both the Atlantic Ocean and the Gulf of Mexico, it had drawn winter vacationers for decades. But by the early seventies, demand for its subtropical amenities had become so strong that recreational development spread North into coastal Georgia, and South and North Carolina.

Not all tourist attractions depend on the resources provided by nature. When the 27,000-acre Walt Disney World Magic Kingdom opened its gates in Orlando in 1971, it brought additional millions of out-of-state visitors to south-central Florida. Many other new attractions were also drawn to this part of the state, especially around Orlando, by the tourist traffic and expenditures. Disney World immediately became the biggest employer in the Orlando area with a total workforce of 51,000. The Disney property development juggernaut also turned this obscure Florida city into the vacation kingdom of the world. The park quickly became an international destination and point of recognition, proving that the South had come of age.

The state's image also made Florida's development efforts easier for it could maintain an air of sophistication as well as mystery for those considering its alluring array of opportunity. Its influx of migrants and retirees gave it diversity. For industry in search of a location, Florida's conservatism and racial moderation lessened the likelihood of criticism or boycott by a civil rights organization. By the end of the 1960s, Florida's rapid gains and bright future made it an industrial paradise, even though it was not in the geographic heartland.

But to truly follow in Florida's footsteps, the rest of the South would have to attract consumer-oriented companies. This became one of the focuses of Southern economic developers. They began to actively promote the fact that many Southern locations could provide access to Florida's burgeoning population without sacrificing connections to mid-Atlantic, Northeastern, or Midwestern markets.

Air conditioning made the sales job easier just as it had already made the region's humid summers bearable. Meanwhile, every developer was quick to remind prospects that winters in any Southern state were far better (warmer, sunnier, and with less snow) than in the Northeast or Midwest. All one had to do is to mention a snow shovel and being cooped up in the house for days on end to light a prospect's fuse.

Along with the geographic and climatic advantages, the South's move toward racial equality sweetened the sales pitch. The South's progress in racial integration was significant, especially when viewed against the backdrop of the previous decades. Bitter conflicts in Boston and a number of other Northern cities over issues like busing and open housing further highlighted Dixie's improvement.

After the passage of the Civil Rights Act of 1964, many companies nationwide began to gradually open their doors to minority employees. Government contractors, bound by anti-discrimination and equal opportunity laws, made the greatest inroads in the hiring of minorities.

A transformation in the composition of the black middle class in America occurred most dramatically after 1970, with the number of black professionals rising significantly. This increase had roots in two major changes. The first was the dramatic expansion of opportunities in higher education for African-Americans. The percentage of blacks with more than a high school education rose gradually in the post-World War II era, primarily because blacks migrated to the North where they had greater educational opportunities. Blacks also entered universities as well as professional and graduate schools in large numbers for the first time after 1970.

The second major change occurred in private as well as public sector hiring practices, particularly for white-collar positions. Many employers began to reach out to minority workers, partly out of fear of litigation. Some of the largest minority white-collar gains were in offices that dealt with state and federal agencies, and that enforced anti-discrimination laws. Employers also began to seek diverse workforces as they realized that multicultural workplaces offered competitive advantages.

Another boost for the South's economy in the 1970s came when Georgia's Jimmy Carter became the first "deep South" President in decades. Carter's presidency brought international attention to the South as a business location that offered affordable land and labor, as well as a great work ethic. Carter's vocal support of equal rights also brought major progress for the South's economy. Suddenly it was "in" to be pro-diversity and vocal about it. Carter was even described as "the triumphant heir of Martin Luther King." When elected President, he took the South by winning 82 percent of its black vote, while losing 53 percent of its white voters. Interestingly, he gained white majorities in only Georgia, Arkansas, and Tennessee.

A successful peanut farmer from a small town, Carter lost his first race for Georgia governor in large part due to his support of African-American rights. This loss was bitter on a personal level. The winner, Lester Maddox, was an ultra-conservative who had gained national media attention by proudly refusing to allow blacks to enter his Atlanta restaurant in direct defiance of desegregation. Maddox had also made headlines for distributing axe handles to his white patrons as a symbol of his refusal to comply.

Determined to overcome this defeat, Carter immediately began positioning himself for the 1970 gubernatorial race. He campaigned endlessly in every corner of the state on a platform calling for an end to busing as a means to overcome segregation in the public schools.

But *The Atlanta Constitution* refused to endorse him. The newspaper called him an "ignorant, racist, backward, ultraconservative South Georgia peanut farmer." Even so, he was able to draw enough votes to force a runoff election, which he subsequently won. In his inaugural address, the new governor surprised many Georgians and received national attention by calling for an end to segregation. Then, during his term in office, he increased the number of blacks serving in state government by 25 percent.

Following Carter's successful 1976 run for the White House, the media proclaimed a resurrected, triumphant South. A larger-than life and more-attractive-than-life South duly appeared in *Time* magazine and *The Saturday Review*, which proclaimed "the South as New America."

Even the traditionally judgmental *New York Times* welcomed the South back into its good graces in February 1976, gushing over the fact that every Southern city has "some transplanted Yankees who have adopted opened collars" and that native Southerners had begun "experimenting with skis."

As the region's peculiarities became more intriguing as well as alluring, a new Southern mystique emerged. While enduring racial problems, below-average pay scales, and the ugly effects of rampant growth were invariably mentioned by the media, the new favorite topic became the amazing reversal of a century-old trend of blacks leaving the South.

During the 1970s, out-migration of blacks from the South reversed. Sociologist Robert Bullard has noted that for the period 1975-1980, over 415,000 blacks moved into the South (U.S. Census South), while 220,000 left the region (for a net immigration of 195,000 blacks). As a result, the region's black population increased by nearly 18 percent. By the end of the decade, it had become home to the largest concentration of blacks in the United States with more than 14 million—nearly one-fifth of its total population. In six of the Southern states, the black population exceeded 20 percent of the total (35.2 percent in Mississippi, 30.4 percent in South Carolina, 29.4 percent in Louisiana, 26.8 percent in Georgia, 25.6 percent in Alabama, and 22.4 percent in North Carolina). It's likely that returning African-Americans were being drawn back to the South by hospitality and opportunities as well as family and historical ties.

Southern population growth wasn't limited to blacks. By the end of the seventies the U.S. Census Bureau had expanded its boundaries of "the South" to include 16 states and the District of Columbia. All of the Southern states experienced a positive net in-migration during the 1970s and also grew at a faster rate than the nation as a whole—a factor that had important economic, political, and ecological implications.

During this same period many Americans began to view the United States more from a regional standpoint than a national one. The media began to increasingly describe the Northeast, Mid-Atlantic, and Industrial Midwest as the "Rust Belt" where the bulk of the country's industry was old and rundown.

Attesting to just how polluted the Northeast had become, Cleveland's Cuyahoga River became known as "the river that burned." Just before America entered the 1970s, this waterway gained a reputation as the nation's most polluted when a welding spark ignited surface oil and debris. This fire and other similar events in the "Rust Belt" became a rallying point for cleaner industry. Where would that cleaner industry startup? The South!

In their scathing coverage of the river fire, the media, perhaps unknowingly, supported the South's case that it was a better place to live and work. For instance, a *Time* magazine article dramatized the situation:

"Some river! Chocolate-brown, oily, bubbling with subsurface gases, it oozes rather than flows. 'Anyone who falls into the Cuyahoga does not drown,' Cleveland's citizens joke grimly. 'He decays.' The Federal Water Pollution Control Administration dryly notes: 'The lower Cuyahoga has no visible life, not even low forms such as leeches and sludge worms that usually thrive on wastes.' It is also—literally—a fire hazard. A few weeks ago, the oil-slicked river burst into flames and burned with such intensity that two railroad bridges spanning it were nearly destroyed. 'What a terrible reflection on our city,' said Cleveland Mayor Carl Stokes sadly."

Increasingly, the national media were suggesting that future business investment would move from the colder, now stagnant, decaying North to the warmer, less densely populated, less developed states of the "Sunbelt." But when it moved South, industry had learned its lessons (reinforced by new environmental policies from the federal government) and opted for the most part to construct virtually pollution-free plants. The South's image of industry became much different, much cleaner than the North's.

The descriptive term "Sunbelt" for the Southern states quickly replaced "the South" as the preferred reference. Kevin Phillips had coined the term in 1969 in his writing about the rise of a Republican political majority. However, he had actually described the Sunbelt as the states of Arizona, California, Florida, and Texas—although he did also mention areas in Georgia, New Mexico, and Tennessee.

But it was a 1975 work by Kirkpatrick Sale that made the term "Sunbelt" interchangeable with "the South." Sale wrote about a climate-driven "Southern rim" region that would challenge the "eastern establishment" for future business investment and development. His "Sunbelt" included 13 states—all of the former members of the Confederacy, except Virginia, plus the "two territories with the greatest Confederate sympathy"— Oklahoma and New Mexico.

Although periodic reports of Southern industrial progress had appeared in national media throughout the 1950s and 1960s, the "Sunbelt" reference ushered in widespread media attention to the region's economic recovery and unbelievable growth. The nation finally was recognizing that for the entire post-World War II period, economic expansion in the South had far exceeded the national pace.

But the region's real surge in industrial growth came in the mid-sixties as enough industries moved south to serve the affluent and rapidly expanding Florida consumer market, Cobb notes. This influx finally gave the South the critical mass to accelerate its growth.

The South's industrial progress had slowed population losses by the mid 1950s and another surge of in-migration began around 1970, giving the region (U.S. Census South) an amazing net gain of 2.9 million people between 1970 and 1976. Between 1950 and 1975, the average rate of economic expansion in the South was 4.4 percent annually, as compared to 3.4 percent rate nationally over the same period.

The best sign for the South was the remarkable diversity of the region's broadening industrial base. Between 1970 and 1975 every industrial category except mining grew faster in the South than the nation as a whole. Major corporations, which had first begun moving away from urban areas in the 1960s, continued this trend into the seventies. Their desire to escape the economic burdens of high-cost Northeastern cities remained unchanged. From 1960-1970 an average of almost 11 percent of the nation's Fortune 500 companies headquartered in New York City left town. CEOs were enticed by promises of milder climates, less crime, lower housing costs, larger lawns, shorter, less stressful commutes, and above all . . . an intriguing ambiance. When they came south, they also found land at considerably lower cost levels, which allowed for sprawling office parks and of all things . . . free parking.

Success in relocating manufacturing operations to the South paved the way for the migration of white-collar functions such as engineering, research, and administration. Personnel officers recognized white-collar salaries like those of production workers also were lower in the South than in the Northeast. The continuing migration of millions of families to the Sunbelt also served as a magnet for companies. Population growth ensured more people with higher experience and education levels would be available for management positions. Because they could offer lower wage rates, the South's mid-size cities like Charlotte, Memphis, and Jacksonville became prime targets of corporate migration.

According to James Cobb per-capita incomes increased by 500 percent in the South from 1955-1975, compared to 300 percent nationwide. Median family incomes rose 50 percent in the South from 1965-1975, compared to 33 percent nationally.

With bank assets soaring, the South's traditional lack of sufficient capital became less of a problem, Cobb notes. In particular, Texas was thriving with its own petrochemical economy.

As previously mentioned, incredibly, the South was also claiming roughly 50 percent—that's HALF—of the nation's annual foreign capital investments for a couple of years beginning in the early 1970s. Foreign firms were investing more than $5 billion in the South by 1972, and $8 billion by 1974. By 1978, many Southern states were attracting annual investments of as much as $1 billion from foreign business investors. The two Carolinas and Virginia led the way in plant locations. Petroleum-rich Louisiana surged ahead in terms of the aggregate value of foreign investments. Tennessee also began to garner major foreign direct investment by 1981 when Nissan selected the state for its North American operations.

No Southern state proved more adept at attracting foreign investment than South Carolina though. For nearly a decade the Palmetto State had drawn nearly 40 percent of its total annual industrial investments from outside the U.S. Promoters with the state's Development Board proudly commented that that there was more West German industrial capital in South Carolina than anywhere else in the world except West Germany.

Red carpet, kid-glove treatment was the rule across the Southern states when receiving and briefing foreign industrial prospects. Southern hospitality paid off well. And the foreign investors clearly appreciated the fact that Southern labor showed basically no interest in forming unions or perpetuating an entitlements workforce.

With things going so well by the mid-1970s, Southern development leaders were not surprised when they began to encounter mounting jealousy and resentment that eventually devolved into attempts to undermine Dixie's continued growth. Several well-publicized analyses of the South's economic growth linked it to the demise of the industrial North, according to Cobb. Early in 1976, *The New York Times* began a series of articles connecting the South's population growth to federal spending through such conduits as the TVA and the military.

Coincidentally, at the same time, the Northeast and North Central states were showing unmistakable signs of economic decay. For example, the New York metropolitan area was losing people at the rate of 2,000 per week. Out-migration from other large cities like Chicago, Cleveland, Pittsburgh, and Detroit as well as smaller ones like Allentown, Akron, Grand Rapids, and Evansville was draining the "Rust Belt" of its talent. Things got so bad that a *Business Week* cover warned readers of "the second War Between the States."

The Sunbelt South was definitely luring workers and consumers away from the old "Rust Belt" region (during 1973 and 1974, over 90,800 more workers covered by Social Security moved from 11 Northern states to the Sunbelt South than in the opposite direction). The growth was led by Florida, which boasted an amazing 65.5 percent growth in the first half of the 1970s.

In 1975, a consulting firm released results of a survey that polled companies on the best business climates in America. It ranked eight of the Southern states among its Top 12 using criteria such as corporate, property, income, and unemployment tax rates; worker's compensation payments; welfare expenditures; labor histories; and the extent of pro-management laws.

By the time Jimmy Carter entered the White House in 1976, Bruce J. Schulman writes in *From Cotton Belt to Sunbelt*, research-based high technology industry had become the watchword of the American economy. The South began to prepare itself for the high-tech companies that would come calling.

North Carolina and Texas led a trend away from site-specific industrial recruitment toward efforts to create a high-tech business environment statewide. North Carolina's second-generation microelectronics center, for example, financed with $88 million in public funds and $20 million from participating companies, was among the first of the region's technology incubators.

As industry and jobs relocated to the South in the 1970s, the region was transformed into an economic mecca and naturally job seekers continued to follow. More than 17 million new jobs were added in the South (U.S. Census South) between 1960 and 1985, compared to 11 million jobs added in the West, and a combined total of 13 million jobs added in the Midwest and Northeast. This new prosperity was mainly in metropolitan areas. Competition among Southern cities intensified as communities enhanced their workforces to lure new industries away from other locations.

Growth in the urban South heightened status differences between rich and poor and between blacks and whites. Poverty coexisted with affluence. Although there was a clear propensity to attract clean industries that required highly skilled workers, many communities could not afford to be as choosy. Even when conventionally "dirty" industry (such as paper, chemicals, and waste disposal firms) came South, they built cleaner and more up-to-date plants. Fortunately, this trend ensured that the South would remain the appealing, dynamic "Sunbelt" it had become.

seven

As the South Matures

The 1980s

In its pursuit of success the South took on a "driven" persona by the 1980s.

The economic growth of the region accelerated, built on the foundation laid in the 70s. Although it was not necessarily clear at the time to many, it was now embarking upon its journey to becoming a second automotive corridor.

And if the automotive industry helped drive the South's economy in the 1980s; technology, research and development, emerging service industries, and tourism/recreation were certainly able to tag along for the ride.

As the South attracted the likes of Nissan, Toyota, and Saturn—along with dozens of first-, second- and third-tier automotive suppliers—it paved the way for what was to become the Southern Automotive Corridor. The region also saw efforts to continue industrial diversification, to actively recruit high-tech companies and their high-paying jobs, and to educate and train its workforce to meet the needs.

The population of the South experienced monumental growth, and the diversity of that population made the South both competitive and attractive. The region was a growing, dynamic area of the country, "full of diversity and change," according to the Southern Growth Policies Board, an organization that started in the early 80s to assess the region's strengths and weaknesses and to develop a set of objectives for the future.

States such as Florida grew so rapidly that they had reached or were on their way to attaining "mega state" status. With a population of 11.3 million, Florida was the sixth-largest state in the U.S., and North Carolina's 6.2 million made it the tenth largest. Both were projected to better that ranking over the next 15 years.

The region was a dichotomy, though—home to relatively fast-growing states and to a smaller group of states that had grown slower than the rest of the South or the rest of the nation. While Florida's population from 1980 to 1985 increased an extraordinary 16.6 percent, seven other Southern states—Georgia, Oklahoma, South Carolina, Virginia, North Carolina, Texas, and Louisiana—posted population growth rates above the national average. Mississippi, Tennessee, Alabama, Kentucky, and Arkansas grew more slowly than the nation.

The population of the New South was diverse—with traditionally much higher percentages of African-Americans than the rest of the nation and an influx of internationals, especially Latin Americans.

The growth in international population in the South had been driven partially by a diversification of the manufacturing base, built on the textile industry. Southern states had become experts at proactively recruiting international firms, many of them European, to support the textile industry. In addition, these foreign investments provided a new mix in business operations—adding machinery manufacturing along with sales and service ventures.

International auto manufacturers and their suppliers, not constrained by the idea that automobiles and other vehicles must be manufactured in the Great Lakes region of the United States, sought and still seek the place with the highest number of available, skilled employees and the best-designed infrastructure.

Since the early 1980s, North American newcomers, largely international companies, have discovered the benefits of the Southern region. While the "big three" (Ford, Chrysler, and General Motors) have been loyal to Detroit and surrounding areas, "increasingly, other auto companies looked at the South as a land of opportunity," according to Lindsay Chappell, Mid-South bureau chief for *Automotive News* magazine. "In contrast to the North, they found wide open spaces, abundant skilled labor and positive relationships with government to get things done."

**Auto Manufacturing In
The South During 1980s**

Current (2003) Automobile Assembly Employment

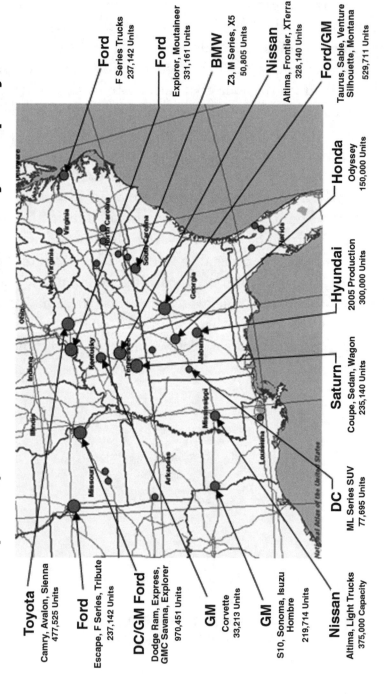

Ford
F Series Trucks
237,142 Units

Ford
Explorer, Moutaineer
331,161 Units

BMW
Z3, M Series, X5
50,805 Units

Nissan
Altima, Frontier, XTerra
328,140 Units

Ford/GM
Taurus, Sable, Venture
Silhouette, Montana
529,711 Units

Honda
Odyssey
150,000 Units

Hyundai
2005 Production
300,000 Units

Saturn
Coupe, Sedan, Wagon
235,140 Units

DC
ML Series SUV
77,695 Units

Toyota
Camry, Avalon, Sienna
477,525 Units

Ford
Escape, F Series, Tribute
237,142 Units

DC/GM Ford
Dodge Ram, Express,
GMC Savana, Explorer
970,451 Units

GM
Corvette
33,213 Units

GM
S10, Sonoma, Isuzu
Hombre
219,714 Units

Nissan
Altima, Light Trucks
375,000 Capacity

By the early eighties, the import market was growing so fast in the U.S. that it became necessary for major international auto manufacturers to establish North American operations.

Tennessee was the first to get into the full-spectrum car-making business, when in 1983 Nissan selected Smyrna for a truck manufacturing facility. That announcement was quickly followed by the good news that General Motors was going to build its Saturn plant near Spring Hill (again in Tennessee!) in 1986. Shortly thereafter Kentucky landed a Toyota plant in Georgetown.

As more international auto manufacturers chose Southern locations, they were followed by hundreds of suppliers that would employ thousands of people across the region.

As the two maps on the preceding pages indicate, the radical growth of mostly foreign but some domestic automotive manufacturing has greatly influenced the economic prospects of the South.

As these shifts occurred, states and communities alike began stepping up their efforts to attract auto-related industries—both primary manufacturers and suppliers.

The South was rapidly shaking its image as a mostly rural region with a less educated, less capable workforce. It had been forced to change that image as the Southern farms began fading and textile operations began giving way to foreign competition. Farmland became prime real estate for the modernization of the South through non-textile manufacturing operations, the service industry, recreational and tourist attractions, and general urbanization.

For example, between 1982 and 1992 Texas lost more high-quality farmland to urban development than any other state (489,000 acres), accounting for 11.5 percent of the total loss in the United States, according to the National Resources Inventory of the U.S. Department of Agriculture. Other Southern states noting a loss of acres of high-quality farmland due to urbanization include North Carolina, Georgia, Louisiana, Florida, and Tennessee. In percent of prime and unique farmland lost, the top 10 states included several in the South: Kansas, Arkansas, Louisiana, Mississippi, and Missouri.

The past decade of the 1970s had been difficult for U.S. farmers. Despite increases in government subsidies, they found themselves increasingly in debt. The decade saw many family-owned farms go into liquidation as the banks foreclosed. The balance in the global food system shifted away from the big food exporters of the Atlantic. Europe and the U.S. were locked in a subsidy war as they tried to keep their farmers in business and competitive in the world market. Japan, the world's most powerful food-importing country, began investing heavily in agro-export sectors abroad.

Thus, a new "global food regime" emerged in the 1980s. The U.S. and others abandoned some of the price supports. Income subsidies and payment for land taken out of cultivation became a major means of appeasing the "farm lobby," but the political influence of farmers was declining.

While affected, the rural, agricultural South used its determination to find ways to deflect some of this impact.

The strong "Bible Belt" work ethic that came with a formerly agriculturally dependent economy proved to be a key advantage, helping the South emerge and begin diversifying its economic base with the help of hardworking, God-fearing people.

To be sure, the South was aware that it had been at a distinct disadvantage in developing high-tech and R&D operations. Since the early 1980s, regional policymakers were increasingly aware that science and technology would provide the key to the region's future. "Toward that end, a wave of science and technology initiatives promoted basic and applied research as well as technology development, innovation and diffusion," reads "Science & Technology Trends in the South," published by the Southern Technology Council in 1989.

While the region's population share grew by 31.4 percent from 1970 to 1986 compared with a growth of only 14.9 percent outside the region, government expenditures for science and technology in the South were dismal.

In 1986, 47 percent of all federal R&D funds went to just four states, only one—Maryland—in the South. Together, though, the four states accounted for only 25 percent of the total U.S. population. Expenditures by the Department of Defense, which funds two-thirds of all federal R&D, were even more concentrated. The same four states received exactly half of those funds.

In addition to resources being unevenly distributed nationally, they also were unevenly distributed within the region. Three Southern states—Alabama, Florida, and Virginia—received 75 percent of the region's federal R&D funds, but accounted for only a third of the region's population. Florida, North Carolina, and Virginia received 60 percent of all industrial R&D funds in the region while accounting for only 40 percent of its population.

Between 1970 and 1986, Southern states lagged behind the national average in their receipt of federal science and engineering funds for universities and colleges, remaining constant at about 15 percent of total funds.

Despite the lack of federal commitment, the South managed to begin building R&D operations and concentrated on research.

North Carolina's Research Triangle, developed in the late 1950s as mentioned earlier, by leaders in business, academia, and industry, grew slowly until 1965 when the appearance of IBM and the National Institute of Environmental Health Services vaulted it quickly onto the national technology scene. By the end of the 1970s, 38 companies had located in RTP, and by 1989, 28 more had added their presence to this flourishing Eastern-U.S.-based hotbed of technology.

In Atlanta, a group of business and civic leaders developed a new type of research operation. They created an independent organization aiding the city in solving its problems through research. "Research Atlanta," as they named the organization, immediately began investigating the effectiveness and efficiency of the Atlanta city government and school system. Other issues tackled would include the environment, water, philanthropy, housing, taxation, and transportation. Today, after more than 30 years in existence, the innovative work done by Research Atlanta has paid off in more ways than I could relate in this book. Strategic public policies have been implemented to encourage minority business development, strengthen tourism, improve schools, bolster the workforce, and undertake numerous other initiatives.

In Alabama officials hoped to emulate the success of Research Triangle Park in their development efforts associated with Oxmoor Valley in the Birmingham area. Over time these efforts would also bear fruit in the form of very diverse industries including representation from aerospace to hi-tech. The University of Alabama's Office of the Advancement of Developing Industries there opened in the mid-1980s, and would go on to support more than $100 million in sales.

Like the University of Alabama, many of the South's colleges and universities increasingly became partners and vehicles for change in the economy.

For example, Georgia Institute of Technology (Georgia Tech) had been around for nearly 100 years by the 1980s, initially the state's centerpiece for industrial growth after the Civil War. Soon, it added engineering and aeronautics and quickly went on to become an internationally prominent research and teaching institution, actively involved in helping the state and the region garner new technological advances while attracting and serving new kinds of manufacturing and business operations. It further developed into a mecca for economic development professionals wanting to hone their skills and become a bigger part of the growth and diversification of the South.

North Carolina State University, also founded in the late 1880s as primarily an agricultural and technical school, emerged as a major research university by pouring millions of dollars into engineering and other research programs. NC State's service-oriented vision and diverse suite of industry-oriented services clearly marked it as a "knowledge economy land grant" institution. The school successfully moved its primary focus from agriculture to industry. In fact, it was an early pioneer of industrial extension service. The university's partnerships have contributed to the growth of the Research Triangle. More recently, NC State established its "Centennial Campus," an ideal marriage between academia and the business world with teaching as well as R&D strongly integrated into the fabric of learning.

Private universities also began to explode onto the scene in the South. Research powerhouses such as Duke and Vanderbilt, specifically known for work in the medical arena, also helped change the South's image.

Institutions like Virginia Tech, Wake Forest, Texas A&M, and Clemson University mimicked the transformation from rural, mostly agricultural and technical schools to those of major stature in research and development, all aiding in the growth of technology in the South and in making the South even more attractive to up-and-coming high-tech industries.

For the South, 1989 was a major turning point in the economic progression from agriculture to manufacturing to technology. That's when the Southern Technology Council issued a report called "Turning to Technology." It was the first regional technology-development plan in the country, and then-U.S. Secretary of Commerce Robert Mosbacher called it "required reading for the rest of the country."

"Turning to Technology" provided further fuel for the state-based tech-development plans that had sprouted in the 1970s and continued in the 1980s. It was a remarkable example of collaboration in a part of the country that practically invented cutthroat economic development competition based on incentives. Though it focused in a comprehensive way on issues that could help the region lure new technology companies, it gave even stronger emphasis to tech growth from within.

The South's focus on technology also made it appealing to high-tech startups that would later become market leaders. For example, in 1984, Michael Dell founded Dell Computer Corp., the first personal computer company to sell custom-made systems directly to end users—a concept that would revolutionize the industry. He chose to base his new endeavor in Texas.

Also taking advantage of the South's 1980s technology climate was an entrepreneur who would create "news until the end of the world." On June 1, 1980, Ted Turner launched CNN from Atlanta. By the end of the decade, the revolutionary 24-hour global news service was viewed in more than 90 countries. Even today, the rest of the world looks to CNN, based in the American South, as its main source for international news.

Just as a side note and solely in my opinion, CNN has probably done more to effect world peace and the spread of democracy in a positive sense than any peace accord, treaty, or foreign aid program. The free exchange of dialogue and open coverage from all over the world that is beamed back to the world has given all of us a better understanding of types of people, forms of government, and cultures. The shining "light" of media coverage that CNN fosters (followed by several competitors) will continue to be a catalyst in building conciliatory policies between nations and will continue exposing rogue governments for what they are.

Another of the South's homegrown companies, FedEx, entered its maturing phase during the 1980s. The air-shipment leader had originally started in 1973 with the launch of 14 small aircraft from Memphis International Airport. The company had selected Memphis, Tennessee, because of its central geographic location and excellent climate, which meant fewer weather-related airport closings. During the 1980s, the growth rate of the company compounded at 40 percent per year. In fiscal year 1983, Federal Express reported $1 billion in revenues and became the first American company to reach that mark within 10 years of startup without mergers and acquisitions.

The increase of jobs in the South from the late 1970s through the 1980s—as well as improvements in the mix of jobs—helped the South raise its overall income level. Eight Southern states raised their per-capita income relative to the nation.

The Southern economy did more than merely match the nation's performance in job growth in the 1980s. Between 1978 and 1997, the South gained 17.7 million jobs. If the regional economy were an exact replica of the national economy in industrial structure and growth rate, the region would have gained only 13.9 million jobs, according to the Southern Growth Policies Board (SGPB).

Going into the 1980s, the South had a very different economic structure than the nation as a whole. For example, the region had disproportionately more jobs in textiles, apparel, chemicals, coal, and petroleum, all of which would grow slowly or decline. Also, the South had substantially fewer jobs in services, a sector that would surge during the 1980s.

While the South did not fully release itself from the grip of its traditional low-wage, low-skill industries; the region diversified and strengthened its competitive position.

The 1980s also saw Southern states place a greater emphasis on helping small businesses flourish. At the start of the decade, small businesses were neither perceived nor recognized for their important role as job-creators. That thinking would dramatically change as MIT researcher and established guru of job creation in America, David Birch, was commissioned by RISEbusiness to quantify the "new job-generation potential" of small business. Birch's work—considered by many to be the seminal, small-business related work of modern times—demonstrated conclusively that the vast majority of new jobs were being created by small businesses.

More than any other single factor, this study changed policy-makers' perceptions of the importance of small business to the economy. It also resulted in many new laws and regulations that were favorable to this sector. According to Birch's 1980s study, enterprises that have less than 100 employees account for roughly 80 percent of new job growth, depending on the business cycle.

The South adopted a proactive stance concerning the new-found importance of entrepreneurs and small businesses.

Public school reforms swept across the South, states upgraded workforce training, and many Southerners "seized expanded opportunities to become entrepreneurs and to prepare for jobs in the shifting economy." More capital became available, and with improved infrastructure and technology, as well as its natural attractiveness, the South was an open range for new businesses and new people.

Even with an increase in service-sector jobs and massive losses in textile manufacturing jobs, the South continued to increase its manufacturing jobs overall. Jobs in durable-goods manufacturing grew, some sectors by as much as 30 percent. For many Southerners, this meant expanded opportunities for high-skill, higher-paying jobs.

The South's cities, now growing into full-fledged metropolitan areas, fueled job growth. Florida, Texas, Georgia, North Carolina, and Virginia saw substantial increases in newly created jobs within their metro areas from 1978 and throughout the 80s, with Florida and Texas leading the charge. In most other states in the region, employment growth in metro areas overshadowed the increases in rural areas.

Although Texas experienced an economic slump due to the energy situation in the early 1980s, its major metropolitan areas comprised of Houston, Dallas, and Austin, continued to grow. Even with the tremendous growth in population and jobs happening in Florida, it would be the Interstate 85 corridor (from Richmond to Atlanta) that would become the newest hotspot for economic growth. The corridor, notes *The Economist* in a 1994 edition, includes North Carolina's Research Triangle Park; some of the South's best universities, including Duke, the University of North Carolina, and Emory; the financial center of Charlotte; the foreign-investment haven around Spartanburg, South Carolina; and Atlanta, the South's biggest city.

Atlanta, home to such corporate giants as Delta Airlines, BellSouth, CNN, and Coca-Cola, like Hartsfield International Airport continued to grow throughout the decade. The 1980s saw significant growth for this Southern market in particular as it labored relentlessly to make itself even more appealing for corporate relocation and business startup.

Like Atlanta, other Southern metropolitan areas became meccas for corporate headquarters, financial institutions, distribution, and tourism—all of which meant jobs. Among them were cities such as Austin, Orlando, Memphis, Boca Raton, Raleigh-Durham-Chapel Hill, and Tampa.

As an interesting aside, Tampa is the only major Florida city not substantially dependent on tourism. It has been sustained by its ties to the airline industry, shipbuilding, and military operations. Still, like many Southern cities, it has enhanced its attractiveness for both residents and tourists with the addition of professional sports franchises.

Many Southern professional sports teams emerged as powerhouses during the 1980s—the Tampa Bay Buccaneers (NFL); the Atlanta Braves (MLB), Falcons (NFL), and Hawks (NBA); the Miami Dolphins (NFL) and Heat (NBA); the Houston Oilers (NFL); the New Orleans Saints (NFL); the Orlando Magic (NBA); the Dallas Cowboys (NFL) —and the list goes on and on. The presence of these franchises has raised the profiles of their respective cities, resulting in additional business growth and development.

All of this—the decline in agricultural and textile jobs; the increase in manufacturing and service sector jobs; a heightened commitment to research and technology; and the drive to build a better, more attractive region—allowed the South to emerge from the 1980s in high gear. As it entered the next two decades it was ready to take on all other regions.

eight

Population Explosion

The 1990s and Beyond

The South has been called "a great seed bed—possibly THE great seed bed of a distinctively American culture; inventing and exporting everything from Coca-Cola to rock and roll."

Add to that fast cars, country music, and Disney World, and by the 1990s, you had a region the whole world recognized as well as looked to for goods and services.

"Urbanization, industrialization and the civil rights movement's successful assault on racial segregation have changed the South's economy and politics beyond recognition," writes John Shelton Reed, Keenan director of the Institute for Research in Social Science and the Louis Harris Data Center at the University of North Carolina, in "The South's Three Personas" published in *The Public Perspective* in 1998. It was Reed who noted the South as "a great seed bed."

The nineties saw the South exploding. It not only had a vibrant and growing population, it also remained as diverse as ever. It was the preeminent hotbed for manufacturing; an incubator for high-tech; the dominant area for international endeavors; evolving into the "seed bed" for service and research; flexing and growing its massive political power; and asserting itself as a mecca for entertainment, cultural events, and sports.

"Southern by the grace of God" is a familiar saying, encompassing not only those who have the Southern birthright, but those who by choice or accident came to call a Southern state their home.

The South in the 1990s again outpaced the nation in population growth. Record-breaking job creation attracted people by the millions. Families began moving south at an even faster rate than companies. As people flowed and continue to flow into the South, the culture became redefined.

Between 1980 and 2000, the South's population (the 17 SEDC states) rose by more than 25 million. The region's population growth rate—30 percent—nearly doubled that of the rest of the nation. Far from its rural roots now, from 1995 to 1997, more than 90 percent of the immigrants to the South moved to a metropolitan area.

The majority of the newcomers came from other regions of the U.S. During the 1990s, about 8.6 million people moved to the South, while only 5.8 million headed out to other regions of the country. Source: U.S. Census Bureau (Populations in Thousands).

Coming full circle, the 2000 Census showed that African-Americans ended the twentieth century by returning to the region. From World War I until the early seventies, African-Americans leaving the South had been one of the great out-migration trends of human history but by the 1990s (and to a smaller degree earlier), the booming new economy and a substantially improved racial climate were drawing them back. Their return in itself was symbolic of the South's resurgence. This migration of African-Americans has become a validation of the tremendous changes in attitude relative to diversity and economic conditions in the South. Southern progress had much to do with its solving of its racial problems. This gave the South the perspective to appreciate the necessity of change.

According to the Census, the South's African-American population in the 1990s increased by 3,575,211; about twice the number the South gained in the 1980s (1.7 million). At the same time, the 1990s was the first decade when each of the other major regions—the Northeast, Midwest, and West, registered a net out-migration of African-Americans. Florida and Georgia led all other states in black gains with Orlando and Atlanta showing the highest growth.

In addition to huge domestic population gains during the 1990s, the South also became a magnet for immigration. The attraction was age-old—people seeking a better life.

"More than at any time since its colonial days, the South has also experienced a rapid growth in foreign immigration—that is, people who moved to the South directly from another country," says The State of the South 2000 report (MDC). Approximately 1.3 million immigrants arrived in the South between 1990 and 1998. The State of the South Report's "South" includes Alabama, Arkansas, Florida, Georgia, Kentucky, Louisiana, Mississippi, North Carolina, Oklahoma, South Carolina, Tennessee, Texas, Virginia, and West Virginia.

Notably, the number of Asian immigrants to the South grew from 52,000 in 1990 to 66,000 in 1996. Meanwhile, the number of legal immigrants from Latin America to the South more than doubled in the first half of the 90s. In 1996, about 138,000 Latinos (mostly residents of Mexico) arrived in the South, representing 55 percent of all legal immigrants to the region, according to The State of the South 2000. By the end of the 1990s, Mexico alone accounted for more than one quarter of all American immigrants, a huge percentage of these in the South.

Fueled by growth in the number of Hispanics along the Mexican border and in its six largest cities, Texas rushed past New York in the 1990s to become the nation's second most populous state behind California, according to 2000 Census figures. The state grew from 16.9 million to 20.8 million in the 1990s. By the end of the decade it had three meccas with more than one million residents, with San Antonio joining Houston and Dallas. It also had three more cities with populations greater than 500,000. Austin, Fort Worth, and El Paso surged past the half-million mark.

As the 1990s ended, we began seeing evidence for the first time that the new immigrant minorities, specifically Asians and Hispanics, were moving to cities that previously had only small numbers of these ethnic groups. Several metropolitan areas and their surroundings tended to be job-generating magnets in the 1990s. The new immigrants found places at both the high and low ends of the economic spectrum.

As far as Hispanics are concerned, Atlanta and Miami, both considered capitals of the "New South," became increasingly popular in the 1990s. Until then, Latinos had an extremely small presence in this portion of the Southern market. As for the remaining Southern metropolitan areas with strong Hispanic gains, Southern Florida as well as South Central Texas increased Hispanic population by more than 50 percent during the 1990s.

Tampa and Oklahoma City increased their Hispanic populations by 40 percent or more, according to Census figures.

Atlanta was also a prominent Asian draw in the 1990s, with this population segment growing by 79 percent. Census figures indicate that Dallas and Houston increased their Asian population by more than half over the 1990s. All of these areas boasted booming economies with rapid job growth in the nineties. The Asian population seemed particularly attracted to regions strong in engineering and high-tech industries—factors in a number of these metro magnets.

The population explosion of the 1990s enabled the South to further strengthen its competitive position and added an ever-growing critical population mass to fuel greater industrial growth.

In the 1990s, Reed points out, 8 of the top 10 states in the growth of manufacturing plants were in the South. From 1992-1994, more than half of the nation's new jobs were created in the South and 10 of the top 13 states in jobs added per 100,000 population were Southern; the top three being North Carolina, Mississippi, and Kentucky.

From 1978 to 1998, nearly four of every 10 jobs gained in the United States were in the South. During the period, the number of jobs increased by 54 percent in the South, versus 38 percent in the rest of the nation. At the same time, the South saw a 30 percent increase in its population while the population of the rest of the country increased just 16 percent. In every Southern state, the number of jobs per 100 people went up. Four states—North Carolina, Virginia, Tennessee and Georgia—had more jobs per 100 in 1997 than the national average. All this according to "The State of the South 2000," a report by MDC, Inc.

"When the nation goes on an economic roll, as it has for much of the 1990s, it takes the South along for the ride," the report notes. "But . . . the Southern economy did more than merely match the nation's performance in job growth in the 1980s and 90s . . . ."

Though it began the previous past two decades with a disadvantageous business-sector mix; the Southern economy now more than matched national growth. According to Dun & Bradstreet, between 1991 and 1995, the South was leading in total net gain in business migration. Businesses also failed less often in the South during the 1990s. According to U.S. Department of Commerce 1996 Statistical Abstract, the percentage of new business failures was only 7.2 percent in the South for the time compared to 9.7 percent in the Northeast, 8.3 percent in the Midwest, and 20.3 percent in the West.

A combination of public policies and private investments helped the South achieve its economic accolades of the 1990s. State and local governments improved roads, built major airports, and provided modern medical facilities, the report notes. The South began to "remodel its economy" once the "albatross of government sanctioned racial segregation was removed." "Public school reform swept across the region during the 1990s as states increasingly upgraded workforce training. Many Southerners seized upon the expanded opportunities to become entrepreneurs and to prepare for jobs in a shifting economy. Financial institutions provided investment capital. Improved infrastructure and technology, as well as natural amenities, made the South attractive to business and people."

By the end of the twentieth century, the South's longtime dependency on low-skill, low-wage manufacturing—particularly textile-related jobs—had dramatically lessened. Textile employment dropped from 681,000 in 1978 to 488,000 in 1997, while apparel jobs went from 599,000 down to 377,000, according to The State of the South. Together, these segments shed 400,000 jobs in two decades, and 50,000 more of these jobs were lost in 1999.

Such monumental losses can be attributed in large part to the North American Free Trade Agreement (NAFTA), which was passed in November of 1993. As noted earlier, this legislation opened the door for many manufacturers to move to Mexico in search of ultra-low-cost labor, a trend that hit the South particularly hard. Now, we are witness to a further migration to even lower cost producers worldwide; in particular China and to a lesser degree, India and others.

Even so, manufacturing of non-durable goods remained a major source of jobs in the rural South, The State of the South 2000 report says. "In 1997, textiles accounted for nearly four percent of the workforce in North Carolina and South Carolina, as well as two percent in Georgia. More than one percent of the workforce in Alabama, Kentucky, Mississippi, Tennessee, and the Carolinas were employed in apparel. Meanwhile, food processing and paper manufacturing grew in the South, while declining elsewhere."

Competitive pressures and technological advances reshaped the South's manufacturing during the 90s. High-tech processes within manufacturing plants became the standard across Dixie.

The result of the building of the automotive industry that started in the South in the 1980s with Nissan, Toyota, and Saturn was a second U.S. automotive industry cluster based in the Southern Automotive Corridor. By the nineties, the growth had kicked into high gear.

When the Southern automotive phenomenon began in the early 1980s, the import market was growing so fast that it became necessary for major international auto manufacturers to establish North American operations. In quick succession, Nissan, Toyota, Saturn, BMW, Mercedes, Honda, and numerous suppliers chose locations in the South.

One of the most impressive announcements (and highlights) for the Southern Automotive Corridor was Nissan's choice of Mississippi for a $930 million vehicle manufacturing plant in 2001. The company cited factors such as the high-quality workforce, a supportive business climate, a cooperative attitude from government, and a favorable incentive package as reasons it chose Mississippi.

With the selection of Mississippi, Nissan had chosen to keep all of its U.S. manufacturing operations in the Southern Automotive Corridor, a decision that began 20 years ago when the company selected Tennessee for its North American headquarters.

Not to be outdone by their Southern neighbors, states such as Alabama, Kentucky, South Carolina, and many others became extremely attractive to auto manufacturers and suppliers in the 1990s. Alabama, for example, became home to Honda and Toyota engine plants. Then, in 1993, Mercedes-Benz determined that Alabama offered the best location for its first passenger vehicle plant outside of Germany.

BMW, another European automaker known for the highest quality, chose South Carolina for its North American operations in 1992. Prior to choosing Spartanburg county, BMW approached the site selection process with the rigor you would expect of a high-quality, European-based automobile manufacturer. After a painstaking three-and-a-half year process involving the investigation of 250 locations worldwide, the company made the strategic decision to build its "Ultimate Driving Machines" in the South. With the ready-to-work attitude the company found in the South, BMW set a new record for the fastest start-up in automotive history—just 23 months.

As the preferred location for the world's best auto companies, Dixie was becoming increasingly international and high tech. Hands down, it was the top choice for international investment by the 1990s.

A prime example is the economic identity of the Greenville-Spartanburg area of South Carolina. Only a generation ago textiles defined it. Now, the I-85 corridor, as it runs through upstate South Carolina, is sometimes called "America's Autobahn." More than 90 international companies have located facilities in this highly international region, most of them in the 1990s.

Twenty years of foreign investment across the South helped accelerate the region's transition toward durable-goods manufacturing. These investments began to be concentrated in high-productivity industries that require higher skills and pay higher wages—automobiles and tires, chemicals and pharmaceuticals, industrial machinery and electronic equipment.

Near the end of the 1990s, nearly 2 million Southerners worked for foreign-owned firms, which accounted for almost 4 percent of private-sector employment in the South.

According to the MDC report, in the first five years of the 90s, the South garnered 42 percent of all foreign greenfield (plant investment starting from land only) development in the U.S. A variety of reasons led foreign investors in search of profits to the South. Two of the best reasons for these choices were that it enabled these companies to tap into the large U.S. market/population base and because it is less expensive to produce their goods closer to their consumers.

Some growth centers have been built on "sophisticated manufacturing with a high-tech focus and an above-average influx of foreign direct investment," the report continues. "An example is Greenville-Spartanburg-Anderson (South Carolina), where employment growth was substantially above the national average from 1978 to 1997."

Several of the South's new-economy centers in the nineties revolved around trade, such as Miami-Fort Lauderdale, importing capital and talent from Latin America while importing and exporting goods from around the world. Charlotte emerged as an international center of banking during the decade.

"Atlanta and Dallas-Fort Worth, two of the South's booming international metros, combine aspects of manufacturing and trading," the report says. "Both feature major airports that serve as vital logistics centers of linking people and exchanging commerce—and both have built solid bases of new-economy businesses."

Contributing to the globalization of the South were not only the importation of international companies and their technology, along with their jobs, but also the vast increase in exports from the region.

While having to play "catch up" with the rest of the nation that had seen a surge in exports in the 1970s, the South increased its exports at a faster pace than the U.S. as a whole in the 1980s and 90s. From 1987 to 1997, the value of exports from Southern states went up from $48 billion to $153 billion—an increase of 221 percent, compared to the U.S. increase of 181 percent. Every Southern state of the (State of the South states) except Louisiana increased exports as a percent of its gross state product in that time period. Among the products exported were the "old standbys" of agricultural and food products, tobacco and cigarettes, and coal and petroleum. That mix also began to include industrial machinery, including computers, electrical equipment, chemicals, and transportation equipment.

While employment shifts within manufacturing in the South have been striking, a more noteworthy trend has seemed to be taking place outside the factories. The trend was seen in the "big-box appliance stores, in restaurants in tourist towns, in offices of glassy skyscrapers, and in hospitals and assisted-living centers," according to The State of the South 2000.

While service jobs doubled nationally from 1978 to 1997, they continued to grow even faster in the South. By the end of the 1990s they accounted for 29 percent of the region's employment. Retail sales represented the second-largest employment sector, behind services, in the South. By the end of the 1990s, the South had as many retail jobs in relation to its population as the U.S. as a whole—9.9 jobs per 100 people.

With this shift in employment segments, the South's "new-economy cities" began to emerge even faster onto the national and global scenes.

Austin and Raleigh-Durham-Chapel Hill were among the fastest-growing centers in the South from 1978 to 1997. Both are knowledge-intensive cities, and are home to major research universities and businesses attracted to or created by the wealth of talent. An emerging trend in the 1990s, industry began to look at "centers of thinking" as standout locations.

The driving factors for locating new high-technology companies during the 1990s became proximity to similar companies, proximity to research universities, and proximity to venture capital. Also factored in, to a lesser degree, were cost of labor, cost of investment, and cost of operations. Once technology clusters reached their limits in terms of resources and capacity, successful firms looked elsewhere.

The South as a whole had planned as well as prepared for these trends. Several of its cities had already proven themselves as incubators for high-tech companies by the 1990s. Locations like Austin and Dallas, Atlanta, Research Triangle (N.C.), Orlando, and Huntsville (Ala.) surfaced as frontrunners of the nation's "new economy" growth.

Other Southern locations also had the inherent qualities high-tech firms were seeking in the 1990s—Hampton Roads and Richmond, Va.; Tampa and Jacksonville, Fla.; Kansas City; Charlotte, N.C.; Birmingham, Ala.; and Knoxville and Nashville, Tenn. Among those characteristics were an available, quality workforce, university relationships and support, state and community incentives, low investment costs, taxes, and quality of life.

Perhaps most importantly, these communities and others across the South were eager to lure tech-intensive firms. Many Southern states had initiatives and programs to take advantage of the high-tech wave of the 1990s. For example, the South Carolina Technology Alliance, a public/private partnership, helped develop legislation that shaped policies for improving the state's workforce, stimulating high-growth businesses, changing tax and regulatory policies, and improving the links between researchers and industries.

The Georgia Research Alliance invested $276 million to create an innovative infrastructure. One of its programs brings world-class researchers to endowed positions at Georgia universities. Another offers funds and research facilities and equipment.

Indeed, in the 1990s, states in the South realized the importance of working together to cultivate a technology base. This new philosophy was built on ideas from reports of the Commission on the Future of the South. "If each Southern state commits itself to raising its sights and assessing its progress," the 1992 report proposed, "we will achieve as a region what few individual states have even attempted." Added to the report in 1998, "To build our competitive position, we need to build broader economic partnerships. No state . . . can afford to go it alone."

While the burgeoning economy of the 1990s fostered some great markets—Atlanta, Houston, and Dallas—and a number of smaller metropolises like Raleigh, N.C., Columbia, S.C., and Richmond, Va.; the real story was in the growth of the Southern suburbs. These suburban enclaves, places like Cary, N.C. (which by the way has been referred to as a "containment area for relocated yankees"), Cobb County, Ga., and Plano, Tex., are home to predominantly middle-class white residents.

Indeed, many of these suburban dwellers are not from the South. By the 1990s, in some booming counties like Wake County, N.C. (home of Raleigh), a large number of the residents were out-of-staters, many of them the once-dreaded Yankees.

As its cities became more alluring for families and businesses, one event in particular helped the South explode onto the world scene in the 1990s. During the Olympic Summer Games of 1996, all eyes were on the South.

"Imagine the chutzpa it took for Atlanta to try to capture the 1996 Centennial Olympic games," says Bruce Adams in his 1998 text *From Boundary Crossers: Case Studies of How Ten of America's Metropolitan Regions Work*. "Many believed they should be held in Athens, Greece, not Georgia. Only two other American cities had ever hosted the summer games—St. Louis in 1904 and Los Angeles in 1932 and 1984. 'People thought I was nuts,' explains Billy Payne, the college football star turned real estate lawyer who in 1987 got the idea to go for the gold. Three years later, on September 18, 1990, with the help of Atlanta Mayor Andrew Young, who is highly regarded in the international community, Atlanta was awarded the games."

Atlanta used the games as a springboard into the twenty-first century. The event left a lasting legacy for the city—and gave every country in the world a first-hand, up-close look at the "New South." The sense of pride experienced resounded throughout the entire South, as the Olympics became an example of what can happen when a community pulls together. Other Southern cities now began to aggressively pursue their unique opportunities.

Along with its other impressive gains, as stated previously, the South became a solid political power in the 1990s. Amazingly, by this decade the region had become overwhelmingly Republican (the party of Lincoln and the Union!).

"What makes this achievement so remarkable and so significant for America's future is the South's political past," *The Economist* says. "For almost a century after the end of Reconstruction in the 1870s, Southern politics was one of America's great certainties. To white Southerners the Republican Party was the enemy. The Democratic Party was a cornerstone of every white Southerner's life." But during the 70s and 80s, a great number of conservative Southerners felt that the national Democratic Party had abandoned them.

Massive numbers of white Southerners finally felt comfortable calling themselves Republicans during the Presidency of Ronald Reagan in the 1980s. Most interesting perhaps, Southerners by this point seemed to be the most conservative members of the Republican Party.

By the beginning of the twenty-first century, America had elected its third consecutive President from the South (two Republicans and one Democrat).

Along with Presidential success, the Southern Republicans also saw significant congressional wins during the decade. Leading the way was Georgia's Newt Gingrich. In 1992 he and

Texas' Dick Armey set in motion a plan to take over the House; and in 1994, they seized on the initial failures of the Clinton administration, targeted those landslide Republican Presidential districts, and seriously funded strong Republican candidates. For the first time in 12 decades the Republican Party emerged with a net advantage among Southern representatives. Even Bill Clinton in the 1992 election carried only 4 of the 11 Southern states despite being a Deep South Southerner.

As the South's population skyrocketed in the 1990s, it also increased its number of electoral votes increasing its importance in Presidential elections.

What does this mean for America in the twenty-first century? As the South continues its shift to becoming increasingly Republican it naturally follows that the GOP will hold an advantage. This is especially true as the South continues to gain in population and wealth. Amazingly, should a Republican nominee for President sweep the South, he or she would have garnered 195 of the 270 electoral votes needed to win.

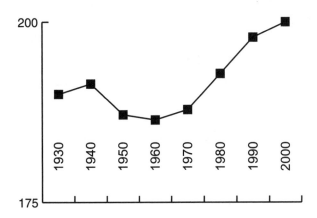

South's Change In Electoral Votes By Decade
1930 vs. 2000

According to *The Economist*, "The inescapable conclusion is that now, largely thanks to the South, Republicans should now win most Presidential elections—as they have since 1964."

Even more importantly, it is my opinion that if the Democrats are serious about winning, a conservative Democrat should win the Presidential primaries for decades, based on the South's electoral vote power, allowing the Presidential elections to be centered on conservative issues and solutions. No matter where early primaries are held, the resulting argument should center on who is electable. That boils down to who can win the conservative Southern states.

By the time the 90's came to a close, the South began to truly see its future. A future that included high-tech growth, cutting-edge research, and fresh, innovative talent . . . all tied together with Southern hospitality and a cultural uniqueness that is hard to resist. The South of 2000 was now a mere shadow of its former self, somehow maintaining its best qualities while shedding those tendencies that had kept it in poverty and darkness. It was being driven forward by its willingness to embrace growth and its ability to ready itself for the challenges ahead.

As it entered the twenty-first century, the South was poised to occupy new a position in America: leadership. It was a long-awaited change from its history and a welcome harbinger of tomorrow.

nine

Southern Leaders

The South's story would not be complete without highlighting several Southern personalities that have helped shape not only our country, but the world.

Life hasn't always been easy for Southerners. As a people, they have been forced to overcome monumental obstacles on their paths to success. It is this struggle, however, that has built character in the men and women who call the South their home.

The strength of Southern leaders (adopted or home-grown), particularly businesspeople and entrepreneurs, is a combination of fierce independence, ingenuity, intellect, and toughness, all tempered with gentility.

The bottom line: qualities learned in Southern life breed strong and oftentimes charismatic leadership. Through the decades, Southern values have persisted in ways that occupations and lifestyles have not. The traits of determination and self-sufficiency, once extolled by Thomas Jefferson, are still imbedded in the character of Southerners.

Many of today's most effective CEOs are Southerners. Their endeavors have helped put the South on the map as a place where individuals and businesses will prosper. As people, they embody the strengths that have put the region in control of its own destiny.

Over the last 50 years, the South has had more than its share of colorful personalities. Its leaders are as brash as CNN-founder Ted Turner in his flamboyant style that mixes bad-boy attitude with good old-fashioned spunk and as quietly effective as Bank of America CEO Hugh McColl. Not all of these leaders were born in Dixie, but each of them had the vision to recognize what the region would become and the wisdom to build their enterprises from a Southern locale.

The South's 180-degree economic change has not happened by accident. It has required direction—the leadership of men and women who are intensely determined to make change happen.

I am including the profiles of a just handful of the many business leaders who have played a major role in the region's success. In taking a closer look at their roots and accomplishments, you'll catch a glimpse of the character qualities that make Southerners a breed all their own.

TED TURNER

> He turned the South into a major media capital.

Wealthy, reckless, voluble, shrewd, funny, flamboyant, altruistic—they're all words that have been used to describe Ted Turner, born Robert Edward III, founder of CNN, TNT, and TBS. He also owns the Atlanta Braves and the Atlanta Hawks and is one of the wealthiest men in the world. Oh . . . one more thing lest we forget; he's also a champion yachtsman.

While Turner is not a native Southerner—he was born in Cincinnati—he has become one of the region's "favorite sons," albeit one who is allowed to get away with his shocking statements about the United States and its leaders, and indeed, the American people in general—once calling us "the dumbest people in the world."

Speaking your mind is, after all, a Southern birthright, even if you often do have to add "bless his heart" after discussing some unfortunate soul.

Ted Turner, "bless his heart," in all his flamboyance and candor, has managed to bring the world into 160 million homes in nearly 40 languages through his pioneering of television's "superstation" broadcasting to cable systems by means of satellite, creating TBS (Turner Broadcasting Station).

When TBS "fused" with Time Warner, Turner became Time Warner's largest shareholder, owning 10 percent of the company. Time Warner is widely known as the largest entertainment company in the world. (His stock was later diluted with the merger of Time Warner and AOL.)

In bringing the world into our homes, Turner has helped bring the world to the South—giving Atlanta a boost as the premier Southern metropolis and creating the Goodwill Games to help bridge gaps among nations.

It all started small. In 1970, Turner took over a struggling, last-place UHF channel in Atlanta, Channel 17. It was producing only the minimal news required by the FCC and had no original programming—opting instead for reruns of old shows and black-and-white movies.

In three years, Turner turned it into a profitable company, and in 1975, it was one of the first stations to gain a nationwide audience. TBS still based itself on those old reruns and movies.

Taking a different direction, a year later Turner bought the Atlanta Braves for $11 million, saving the team and possibly even Atlanta sports in general. One year later, he bought the Atlanta Hawks basketball team.

In 1980, he started what was to become one of the most comprehensive news organizations in the United States and arguably the world. It was this year that he formed CNN, a 24-hour news channel and the first national cable network.

Turner's CNN made huge strides while covering the 1981 Reagan assassination attempt, 1986 space shuttle disaster, and the Iraqi war, which placed reporters in the direct line of fire. Time and time again, CNN reporters were, and still are, always the first ones on the scene.

In 1986, Turner tried unsuccessfully to buy CBS. Instead, he purchased Metro-Goldwyn-Mayer (now MGM/United Artists).

In 1988, Turner began another station, TNT (Turner Network Television). TNT is currently viewed in over 61 million homes across America.

In August 1990, he also launched a network that stretched across the Southeast called SportSouth. The network provides coverage of Atlanta Braves baseball, Atlanta Hawks basketball, college football, auto racing, volleyball, golf, tennis, and other major sporting events. Turner later sold the operation to FOX Sports.

In 1996, Turner finalized a deal with Time Warner. Time Warner was given ownership of TBS and everything under it. On Oct. 10, 1996, he became the vice chairman of Time Warner, Inc. Now he had control of everything he had previously directed plus E! Entertainment and Comedy Central cable television stations.

Through his land acquisitions in the American West, Turner has recast himself as a visionary environmentalist as well as the largest private landholder in the U.S. His Turner Foundation supports environmental programs, such as energy, forest/habitats, water/toxics and population, and donated $1 billion to the United Nations.

He frequently has challenged other wealthy businesspeople to give their money to make a difference. "It's not an obligation," he told the *Atlanta Journal-Constitution*. "It's your money; if you want to make a big pile of it and burn it, you can do it. But what I'm talking about is making an investment in the future of humanity, and how much joy it gives you."

Turner's methods of buying broken-down businesses and improving them, motivating his staff, and building a success pyramid by borrowing and trading stock are a model for all young professionals. He described his methods in *The Ultimate Success Manual*, in which he discusses his tactics and strategies along with his influence on ending the Cold War, with environmental and disarmament groups, and his herds of buffalo with solar fences.

Turner is still very much the skipper of his boat—much like when he captained the *Courageous* to an America's Cup victory in 1977. He is a Southern skipper who has set the tone for others to come.

SAM WALTON

From rural Arkansas, this discounting dynamo created what would become the #1 company in the world in revenues.

His life could be described as an equation: good ideas plus hard work with a few breaks mixed in for good measure equals big results.

Sam Walton always was a student of retailing, even visiting stores during family vacations. When the discounting retail business began emerging in the early 1960s, he was in his 40s and already was a successful businessperson with 15 variety stores across Arkansas, Missouri, and Oklahoma. Prior to this he had felt the sting of failure of failed stores, one occurring from a poorly selected location and the other resulting from a poorly constructed lease. These experiences each contributed to his later success.

When a barber named Herb Gibson began opening discount stores near Walton's variety stores, Walton immediately saw what was coming.

At age 44, he opened his first Wal-Mart in July 1962 in Rogers, Ark., the same year Kmart, Woolco, and Target began.

An investor in local five-and-dimes, Walton had none of the corporate backing or experience of the other three. He did have "a searing insight . . . that small towns could support big stores," Harvard business professor Richard Tedlow told the *Christian Science Monitor*.

Walton took aim squarely at rural America, which ended up being a brilliant strategy. By choosing to not enter the same markets as the other chains, he could experiment quietly in his quest to increase his retail presence that was for the most part off the media's radar screen.

Walton excelled at recognizing and implementing the successful techniques of his competition. He also welcomed the suggestions of his own employees—one in Louisiana suggested the idea of front-door greeters. Once committed to the cause of discounting, Walton began a philosophy that lasted the rest of his life. His company would drive down costs throughout the merchandising system, allowing consumer prices to go down.

Walton was born on March 29, 1918, near Kingfisher, Oklahoma. His family owned and lived on a farm until 1923. He attended the University of Missouri, majoring in economics.

After graduating and his military service, he began his career as a retail merchant when he opened the first of several franchises of the Ben Franklin five-and-dime in Arkansas.

In his Wal-Mart endeavors, Walton always used his vision to keep his stores ahead of the curve. For example, he was among the first to use information to his competitive advantage. After attending an IBM school in 1966 (when he had just 20 stores), he knew computerization of merchandise controls was imperative to his company's growth. He also realized early on the power of the bar-code scanner to automate inventory. Wal-Mart became a model for just-in-time inventory control and sophisticated logistics, and today the chain's computer database is second only to the Pentagon's in capacity. From the South, Walton became the first true information-age CEO.

Along with his tremendous vision, Walton's management style was popular with employees and helped to spur growth, as he took the company public in 1970. The decentralized distribution system created the edge needed to further impel growth in the 1980s amidst growing complaints that the "superstore" was squelching smaller, traditional Mom and Pop stores.

Through the years, his greatest achievement may have been allowing his down-home attitudes to shape corporate culture. Every customer was important and treated as such. He instituted a 10-foot rule where employees are supposed to greet customers whenever they get within 10 feet of them. Incredibly frugal, Wal-Mart's main offices even today look more like an old, outdated mall than the headquarters of the world's largest company in terms of revenue.

As he preferred, Walton spent most of his life sheltered from the limelight. Few people had heard of him when *Forbes* magazine determined in 1985 that he was the richest man in America.

When the media did pay attention to Walton, it was more his preference for pickup trucks over limos (as you would expect from a true Southerner!).

By 1991, Wal-Mart was the largest U.S. retailer with 1,700 stores. Walton remained active in managing the company, as President and CEO until 1988 and chairman until his death in 1992. By the way, it was not unusual for Sam to "swoop down" out of the skies in his little aircraft on any given day to visit several stores. There is an often repeated story about an unscheduled visit to a Sam's location in Corpus Christi, Texas, just to let the new store's team know he was around to help. After filling in for a stocking clerk for about an hour, he gathered the staff, thanking them one by one for making his vision of Sam's Club a reality.

Sam Walton's venture has become the world's largest multi-national revenue-based corporation. At the time of this writing, approximately 100 million people shop at a Wal-Mart each week. And the company's annual sales rival the gross domestic product of Austria.

From the South, innovator Sam Walton built the most successful retail business in history. And in doing so, he forever impacted the marketing culture of the entire world.

FRED SMITH

From Memphis, he revolutionized overnight shipping.

Fred Smith is responsible for starting what is arguably one of the most recognizable names in the world—Federal Express, now FedEx. The company spawned an industry of overnight package delivery services, won the first Malcolm Baldrige National Quality Award in the service category, and ranked among the top ten of "The 100 Best Companies to Work for in America" in the early 1990s.

What is today a major operation, shuffling millions of packages around the globe on a daily basis, all began in 1965, when Smith was a Yale undergraduate. He wrote a term paper proposing an air-freight system that could accommodate time-sensitive shipments such as medicines, computer parts, and electronics. To be effective, his system would have to function at night. Federal Express officially began operations on April 17, 1973, with the launch of 14 small aircraft from Memphis International Airport—in the heart of the South.

Smith himself has described the original concept of FedEx as being "built around moving very high-priority parts for the electronic and medical industries. When you have one of those parts, and a computer is down, or a hospital is in need of something, you really have to do what you say you're going to do." That idea became such a part of the cultural fabric of the company that now it's essentially self-perpetuating.

In his management style, Smith tells his executives, "Spend time on the high-leverage activities, and delegate those activities that aren't high-leverage."

He told *Fast Company* magazine, "My leadership philosophy is a synthesis of the principles taught by the Marines and every organization for the past 200 years.

"When people walk in the door, they want to know: 'What do you expect out of me?' 'What's in this deal for me?' 'What do I have to do to get ahead?' 'Where do I go in this organization to get justice if I'm not treated appropriately?' They want to know how they're doing. They want some feedback. And they want to know that what they are doing is important.

"If you take the basic principles of leadership and answer those questions over and over again, you can be successful dealing with people. The thing that I think is missing most in business is people who really understand how to deal with rank-and-file employees."

Today, Smith is Chairman, President, and CEO of FedEx Corporation, the entity that encompasses all FedEx operating companies.

With annual revenues of $20 billion plus, FedEx Corporation is the premier global provider of transportation, e-commerce, and supply-chain management services. The company offers integrated business solutions through a network of subsidiaries operating independently, including: FedEx Express, the world's largest express transportation company; FedEx Ground, North America's second largest provider of small-package ground delivery service; FedEx Freight, a leading provider of regional less-than-truckload freight services; FedEx Custom Critical, the world's largest provider of expedited time-critical shipments; and FedEx Trade Networks, a provider of customs brokerage, consulting, information technology, and trade facilitation solutions.

Decades earlier, Fred Smith anticipated the needs of twenty-first century business. From the South, his company FedEx has increased the speed of commerce, forever changing the way business gets done. Now, when it absolutely, positively has to be there, America turns to FedEx, one of the South's homegrown ideas and companies.

WILLIAM H.G. "BILL" FRANCE

He made NASCAR big business.

"The Man" who *was* stockcar racing! That's how NASCAR founder William H.G. "Bill" France is remembered.

While he didn't invent the sport, he was responsible for organizing it and making it "more palatable than the slipshod, fly-by-night enterprise it had been until he came along," wrote the *Daytona Beach News Journal*.

"Big Bill," as he was known, took stockcar racing to a whole different level, imposing his big stature along with his big ideas on those with whom he interacted.

"It was more than just organization, which he officially brought to the sport with that 'constitutional convention' atop Daytona Beach's Streamline Hotel in December 1947," the *News Journal* writes. "No, when people reflect on Big Bill, the word that keeps coming up is vision."

A stockcar driver in the 1930s when the sport began with relatively informal competition, France called an organizational meeting of car owners, drivers, and mechanics in late 1947 to establish racing standards and regulations.

The meeting was held at Daytona Beach, Fla., the site of a popular track, part sand and part road. As a result, the National Association of Stockcar Auto Racing was incorporated in February of 1948, with France as its President.

France ruled NASCAR from that point until 1972, building stockcar racing into the richest, most popular of all motor sports. The 6-foot-5 France was often called a dictator. In response, he once smiled and said, "Well, let's make that a benevolent dictator. What I'm doing is best for the sport, not just me."

In 1959, France opened Daytona International Speedway, the first so-called "super-speedway"—a 2.5-mile, high-banked oval and the site of NASCAR's most prestigious race, the Daytona 500. By building it in Daytona, he signaled that the days of beach racing were over. Within the next decade, other super-speedways were built at Atlanta, Charlotte, Dover, Michigan, Pocono, and Rockingham. France opened another super-speedway, the 2.66-mile oval at Talladega, Ala., in 1969.

When members of the newly-established drivers' organization, led by Richard Petty, proposed boycotting Talladega because tires might not be able to handle its 195 mile-per-hour speeds, France borrowed a car and did several laps at 176 miles an hour. "Surely the young pros can run 20 miles an hour faster than I can," he said, and the boycott fizzled.

Through his keen foresight and vision, Bill France turned a sport he loved into a major industry. His leadership gained for NASCAR a devoted following—first in the South, then in all of America.

HUGH MCCOLL

> He was instrumental in making Charlotte a world-class financial center.

Under Hugh McColl's tenure as chairman and chief executive officer of Bank of America, headquartered in Charlotte, N.C., the bank went from $12 billion in assets to $610 billion in assets. Through more than 100 mergers, the bank has grown from a local North Carolina bank to one of the largest in the United States.

In Charlotte, McColl's influence was key in making the city a regional powerhouse of industrial growth and business. The Bank of America building in downtown Charlotte has been described as a symbol of the city's prosperity and the bank's presence there has firmly established Charlotte as a major financial center.

When McColl became chief executive of its predecessor NationsBank in 1983, the bank had $12 billion in assets, $8 billion in deposits, and a market capitalization of $700 million. The company operated in two states, employed 7,600 associates, and generated net income of $92 million.

Fifteen years later, Bank of America had $595 billion in assets, $346 billion in deposits, $47 billion in shareholder' equity, operating income of $6.5 billion, and a market capitalization of about $100 billion, making it one of the most highly valued financial services companies in the country and in the world. By 2002, the company was operating branches in 22 states and the District of Columbia, employed almost 180,000 associates, had relationships with 30 million households, and served two million businesses in the U.S. and 37 other countries.

McColl successfully built the company into a model for financial services. The bank is a technology leader, and was one of the first to offer services through personal computers and the telephone. Bank of America serves commercial and institutional clients through a worldwide network of corporate finance and investment banking offices.

Acting on the conviction that his company's health depends on the health of its communities, McColl has led Bank of America to reinvest its resources across the franchise. Bank of America has committed to investing $350 billion in economically underserved communities. The company also is recognized as the nation's leader in expanding relationships with companies owned by minorities and women.

Under McColl's direction, Bank of America also broke new ground in helping associates lead balanced, healthy lives. Through its Volunteer Time for Schools initiative, Bank of America grants associates up to two hours of paid time each week to volunteer in local schools. *Working Mother* magazine has honored McColl and Bank of America for the company's progressive work-and-family programs.

McColl was born June 18, 1935, in Bennettsville, S.C. He earned a bachelor's degree in business administration at the

University of North Carolina at Chapel Hill in 1957. After serving as an officer in the U.S. Marine Corps, he joined Bank of America's predecessor in 1959 as a management trainee. Within 15 years, he was named president of the bank. In 1983, he was elected Chairman, President, and Chief Executive Officer of the corporation.

Retiring from Bank of America in April 2001, McColl didn't sit idly by. He started McColl Partners LLC. This investment-banking firm offers merger and acquisition services for their target clients—companies in the financial services, healthcare, technology, and manufacturing sectors with annual revenues of $250 million or less.

Through his strong leadership of Bank of America, Hugh McColl helped transform the once capital-starved South into a global financial center.

F. KENNETH IVERSON

From the South, he revolutionized the steelmaking industry.

F. Kenneth Iverson took a failing nuclear instruments company and turned it into a revolutionary steel manufacturer, the Charlotte, N.C.-based Nucor. Under Iverson, Nucor became known world-wide as one of the most daring and innovative manufacturers in any industry. Iverson cultivated a culture where employees keep setting productivity records that are the envy of the steel industry. He also has spurned textbook formulas, defied Wall Street, and refused to create a mission statement—all character-istic of the independent Southern spirit!

Today his company, Nucor Corp., is the king of the mini-mill producers and is the second-largest steelmaker in America, just after USX Corp.'s U.S. Steel Group. Headquartered in Charlotte,

N.C., Nucor produced 9.72 million tons of steel last year—up 15 percent from the year before—slipping past Bethlehem Steel Corporation and LTV Steel Co., Inc., into the No. 2 spot. By one estimate, Nucor has accounted for 83 percent of the U.S. steel industry's growth in shipments during the last decade.

That achievement is particularly remarkable because when Iverson joined the company in 1962, it didn't make any steel at all. The firm (then known as Nuclear Corporation of America) had just ventured into the steel-fabrication business by acquiring Vulcraft Corporation, a manufacturer of construction joists, and hired Iverson to run the new unit.

In 1966, a year after being appointed company president, he persuaded the board of directors to invest in steelmaking operations—arguing that the firm would save money by producing its own steel for joist fabrication. The company's first mill, in Darlington, S.C., went on line in 1969. In retrospect, that event can be regarded as a turning point that ushered in the modern era of electric-furnace mini-mills that have revolutionized the steel industry.

Nucor, which as of 2002 had eight steel-producing mills as well as a number of steel-fabrication businesses, experienced phenomenal growth during the previous three and a half decades. In 1964, the year before Iverson became president; its sales were just $17.5 million. But in 1997, Nucor's revenues totaled $4.18 billion—representing a 15 percent gain from 1996 and a whopping 23,811 percent increase in 33 years. As it entered the twenty-first century, Nucor ranked 422nd on *Industry Week's* list of the world's 1,000 largest publicly held manufacturing companies.

A Southerner by choice, Iverson was born September 18, 1925 in Downers Grove, Illinois, a rural town west of Chicago. He served in the U.S. Navy from 1943 to 1946, rising to the rank of lieutenant. He earned a bachelor of science degree in aeronautical engineering from Cornell University and later he received a master's degree in mechanical engineering at Purdue University.

Over the next three years, as Vulcraft tripled sales and profits, the rest of Nuclear Corporation was losing money so quickly that the company was headed toward bankruptcy. In 1965, Sam Siegel, a corporate accountant for the company, resigned but sent a telegram to the board saying he would reconsider if the board named him treasurer and Iverson President. The board, desperate to save the company, agreed.

Iverson and Siegel, along with a manager from Vulcraft named David Aycock, together would lead Nucor over the next three decades. Iverson almost immediately moved the company to Charlotte and jettisoned its money-losing operations to focus on Vulcraft. Iverson soon felt that Vulcraft was vulnerable to changes in the price and supply of steel to make its steel products. Iverson and the board decided the company would make its own steel from a new plant in Darlington, S.C., that opened in 1969.

Under Iverson's leadership, Nucor created a joint venture with a Japanese steelmaker at a time when anti-Japan sentiment was high in the U.S. steel industry. Within a decade of its mid-1980s beginning, that venture, Nucor-Yamato, had become the dominant producer of wide-flange beams for construction in the United States.

Under Iverson's leadership, Nucor proved that even industries steeped in Northern tradition could thrive in the American South.

ROGER MILLIKEN

His commitment to quality has made his company a textile leader.

"Good is the enemy of best and best is the enemy of better," says Roger Milliken, CEO of Milliken & Company. With this attitude, Milliken has created a "we-can-learn-from everyone" corporate culture at his South Carolina textile company.

Roger Milliken was the lightning rod in helping Milliken & Co. become one of the world's largest privately held corporations. With more than 1,500 patents, it manufactures diverse products from finished fabrics for uniforms and spacesuits to textiles for tennis balls, napery items, automotive fabrics, and sails. Milliken Carpet is a world leader in the production of rugs and carpets for residential, commercial, and institutional uses. The company also makes specialty chemicals that are used in dyes, plastics, and petroleum products.

Early on, just after World War II ended, Milliken observed that the Italians and Germans had developed a very sophisticated, state-of-the-art textile machine. These new machines would clearly provide him with an edge that would later result in his taking the industry by storm. The key to expanding this success into an economic recruitment engine was Dick Tukey's (a recruiter and friend) insistence that Milliken buy the machines only if there was an adequate U.S. sales and service force and that they locate on I-85.

Firmly focused on superior quality, Milliken has motivated his employees to look outside their work groups, business units, and corporation for ideas to continuously improve performance. Under his powerful leadership, in 1990 his company became the recipient of the prestigious Malcolm Baldrige National Quality Award.

To drive quality improvement, Milliken has built a corporate culture that encourages information sharing and idea exchange among all team members, even the CEO. He personally is known to stay late at the office and on occasion he works late with associates on detailed projects. He has no doors on his office, shuns corporate parking spaces, executive dining rooms, and other perks that might separate him from the team he leads.

A strong supporter of education, Roger Milliken has translated his belief in lifelong learning into strong educational initiatives within Milliken & Company. Milliken University, located on Milliken's corporate campus, has 15 dedicated classrooms devoted to maintaining the highest level of job skills and the goal of a well-educated workforce.

Born in New York and a Yale graduate, Milliken is recognized nationally and internationally for his lifelong commitment to excellence, innovation, leadership development, environmental protection, and continuous quality improvement in every aspect of the field of textiles.

H. ROSS PEROT

From the South, this self-made billionaire businessperson also made some waves in politics.

Our list of influential Southern leaders simply wouldn't be complete without this colorful Texan.

Colorful? Just listen to what Ross Perot told the *Dallas Morning News* when asked in 1981 to write his own epitaph: (He) "made more money faster. Lost more money in one day. Led the biggest jailbreak in history. He died. Footnote: *The New York Times* questioned whether he did the jailbreak or not."

There's no question Ross Perot embodies Southern leadership. His very distinct personality has given him the independence and courage to envision huge things and actually make them happen. Perot has been described as a great motivator and a man who demands loyalty and hard work from employees. But as his employees would likely attest, he often repays that hard work with acts of great generosity and charity.

From his boyhood in Texarkana (where he was born in 1930), Perot was diligent and entrepreneurial. Beginning at age seven, he worked at odd jobs including breaking horses; selling Christmas cards, magazines and garden seeds; delivering newspapers; and collecting for classified ads.

Later came his biggest business venture of all. In 1962, his schoolteacher wife loaned Perot $1,000 from her savings to start a one-man data processing company, which he named Electronic Data Systems. In 1964, the company made $4,000 out of $400,000 in revenues. By 1968, it had grossed $7.5 million and made a profit of $2.4 million. Today EDS is a multi-billion dollar corporation employing more than 70,000 people.

Perot sold EDS to General Motors in 1984 for $2.5 billion, though he remained on the board of directors until 1986. Always energetic and inventive, Perot started another business venture in 1988 called "Perot Systems" (Another computer-data-driven company).

Along with his successes in the business arena, Perot has served state and federal governments in varying capacities. In 1969, he partnered with the U.S. government to help improve the brutal treatment American POWs were receiving in Southeast Asia. He worked on the project for four years, placing himself and his family at considerable risk, until the prisoners were released in 1972 at the end of the Vietnam War. For his efforts, he received the Medal for Distinguished Public Service, the highest civilian award presented by the Department of Defense.

In the late 1970s, the governor of Texas requested this Southerner's assistance in dealing with the problem of illegal drug use in the state. Perot led the Texans' War on Drugs Committee, which saw five anti-drug bills become law.

In 1982, another Texas governor asked for Perot's assistance to improve the quality of public education in the state. Recognizing that a quality educational system is the key to economic development, Perot led the effort to reform the school system. The result was big-time legislative changes and improvements in Texas public schools.

By the 80s, President Ronald Reagan had called on Perot to join the President's Foreign Intelligence Advisory Board, a little known highly powerful group of appointees whose approval is required for all U.S. covert operations worldwide.

But Perot's biggest foray into the world of government came in his run for the U.S. Presidency in 1992, in which he garnered 19 percent of the vote. In my opinion, every American owes Perot a "thank you" for spending so much of his personal money in his run for President because it resulted in Americans understanding what federal budget deficits were doing to undermine the country's success. Whether or not you agree that Ross Perot was the right messenger, his message is sound. Until then, both political parties had just paid lip service to the deficits.

Later, he founded the organization United We Stand America to promote his agenda—denouncing big government, budget deficits, campaign finance practices, and the two-party system. Subsequently, he organized the Reform Party to contest the 1996 Presidential election.

Through it all, Ross Perot characterized the values-driven independence, resilience, and persistence that are so often found in Southern leaders. As he once explained, "Most people give up just when they're about to achieve success. They quit on the one-yard line. They give up at the last minute of the game one foot from a winning touchdown." Not Ross Perot. Not Southern leaders. No way.

ten

Crunch the Numbers

Operating in the South
Equals Lower Business Costs

If you operate a company, I've included here an analysis of business operating costs. If you are an individual, I believe these numbers will make a convincing case that will encourage you to climb a Southern-based career ladder.

Financially, the rewards of one location over another can be powerful and in many cases can literally mean your business' survival! Business operating costs in the four U.S. regions can vary tremendously. To keep competitive and to even stay in business with today's narrow profit margins, it is essential to keep costs as low as possible.

So if you want to create substantial savings for your manufacturing business, consider moving or expanding it to the American South. It is a proven fact that the costs for expenses associated with labor, workers' compensation and unemployment insurance coverages, corporate taxes, and construction or leasing can be dramatically lower than what you may be paying

---

now in any of the other three U.S. regions. In many cases these costs can equate to millions of dollars in annual cost of operations savings.

If you believe we're all wet on this, please read on! To illustrate how a Southern location will improve your balance sheet, we've constructed a case study centering on five expenses and how those expenses compare in the four U.S. regions: South, Midwest, Northeast, and West (this tracks a similar study done by *Southern Business & Development* magazine). The five expenses are payroll (average per region), workers' compensation (average per region), unemployment insurance (average per region), corporate taxes (average per region), and construction costs (average costs to build your facility per region). For the study, we will be comparing these costs for a 100-employee, 100,000-square-foot facility in Standard Industrial Code 37. Final regional tallies can be found at the end of this chapter. We tracked year 2001 data unless otherwise indicated.

While we will be using a manufacturing plant as a unit of measure, this benchmark is reflective of service industries also. Regardless, the profit equation never changes. Lower costs equal higher profits. The South equals lower costs. Running your business in the South equals higher profits.

Labor Costs

Regardless of where you locate your next expansion, you're going to have payroll costs. Other than state income tax liability, very little can be done to offset how much you end up paying your employees in a certain region. Pay too little and you're not going to get the labor quality you need. Pay too much and it will undoubtedly have a negative effect on your bottom line. Pay competitive wages, those that slightly exceed the state average for the type of job you're creating and you'll be well on your way to finding the quality of labor you are seeking along with the proper balance of productivity and costs.

Let's look at average annual pay and average manufacturing wages in the four regions of the U.S. Not surprisingly, as you can see by the chart below, the Northeast leads all U.S. regions in average annual pay with $32,128.

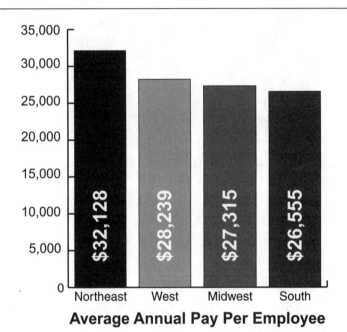

Average Annual Pay Per Employee

Source: U.S. Dept. of Commerce, 1999

Manufacturing Wages

Since this is a manufacturing facility we are using in the study, let's take a look at average manufacturing wages in the four U.S. regions.

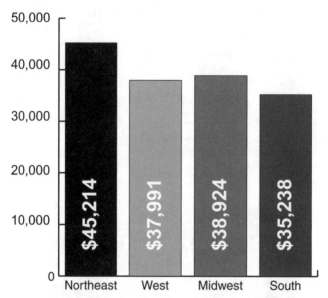

Manufacturing Labor Costs Per Employee
Based on Standard Industrial Code 37

Source: U.S. Bureau of Labor Statistics 2000

Conclusion

As you can see by studying the second chart above, the South features the lowest manufacturing wage of any U.S. region. In fact, the South's average manufacturing annual pay is almost $10,000 less per employee than what employers pay in the Northeast. That's a savings of almost $1 million a year in payroll when operating a 100-employee facility (in Standard Industrial Code 37) in the South as opposed to the Northeast and over the course of five years, the Northeast adds an additional $5 million in payroll costs. In five years your 100-employee Southern-based business will save $1.37 million in payroll when compared to the West and $1.84 million when compared to the Midwest. The disparity is even more glaring when you compare the urban Northeast with the semi-rural South. As a side note, my opinion is that the semi-rural areas in the South offer the absolute best of all worlds. Specifically, this refers to counties contiguous to metropolitan areas that can afford a company the greatest payroll savings with the highest productivity.

You might also be interested to know that Connecticut has the highest annual manufacturing average pay in the U.S. at $56,505 and Mississippi has the lowest with $27,640 (year 2000 figures).

Workers' Compensation Premiums

This might be every company owner's least favorite extra cost item. As you can see by studying the following chart, worker' compensation costs to a company vary greatly with each U.S. region.

By adding each state's annual workers' compensation outlay for a 100-employee company in SICs 35, 36, and 37, we came up with an average per state. Each state's average was then added to the other states in that region to come up with an annual regional average for workers' compensation outlays. It must be noted that in almost every state, workers' compensation costs for SIC 37 are much higher than SICs 35 and 36. This increases each region's annual average above the average of what companies in SICs 35 and 36 would pay annually in workers' compensation. Once again, this difference is greatest among more urban areas of the Northeast and semi-rural areas of the South.

As the chart below indicates, the South really shines in this area. Often overlooked, however, are the hidden costs in longer absences from work by employees receiving these benefits. These include more training for replacements, less productivity from

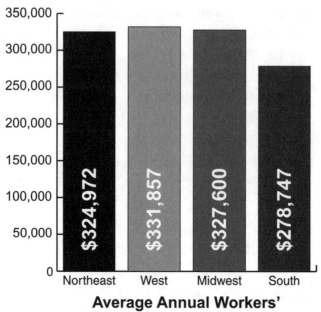

**Average Annual Workers'
Compensation Premiums**

For companies with 100 employees in SICs 35-37. Source: U.S. Dept. of Commerce, 2001

replacement workers, and breeding discontent in the workplace as the result of these unexplained extended absences. The above differences are all subjective and therefore cannot be included in any such tabulation.

Unemployment Insurance Premiums

While not as frustrating and costly as workers' compensation premiums, unemployment insurance is no walk in the park for a business owner employing 100 people. As you can see by the information found in the following chart, unemployment insurance premiums vary widely from region to region.

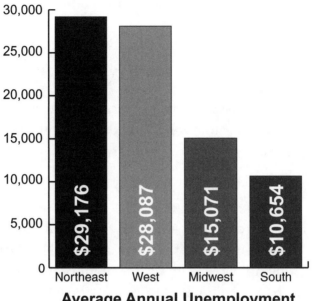

Average Annual Unemployment Insurance Premiums

Source: U.S. Dept. of Commerce, 2001

For a manufacturer employing 100 people in the Northeast, expect to pay, on average, $29,176 annually for unemployment insurance premiums. Unemployment insurance premiums in the West aren't much cheaper than those found in the Northeast for a 100-employee company. In the West you'll pay $28,087 on average annually. It drops significantly in the Midwest where companies employing 100 will pay on average $15,071 annually. It isn't until you look at the South's annual average for a 100-employee operation that you realize just how low these premiums can go. In the South, expect to pay about

$10,654 each year in unemployment insurance for a 100-employee operation.

It must be noted that the Northeast's annual unemployment insurance premium average is skewed by the incredibly high cost of those premiums in Connecticut, New Jersey, and Rhode Island. The same can be said for the West's annual average, which factors in Alaska, Hawaii, Oregon, and Washington's absurdly high unemployment insurance premiums.

Conclusion

Summarizing, on average you'll pay $18,522 more in the Northeast, $17,433 more in the West, and $4,417 more in the Midwest for unemployment insurance premiums each year than you would in the South for a 100-employee business.

Corporate Income Taxes

Corporate taxes run the gamut in the U.S. Some states, such as Texas in the South, Nevada, Washington, and Wyoming in the West, and South Dakota in the Midwest, are free of corporate income tax. On the other hand, states in the Northeast such as Connecticut, Massachusetts, New Jersey, New York, Pennsylvania, and Rhode Island tax corporate revenues nine percent or more.

The following chart shows an average corporate state tax rate for each region of the U.S. We have gone further to show the total average annual corporate tax expenditure per region for a 100-employee manufacturing operation theoretically grossing $10 million each year, without regard to certain states' income thresholds, levels, or write-offs.

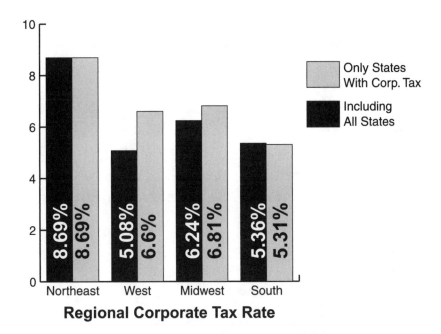

Regional Corporate Tax Rate

Regional corporate tax rate only factoring in states that have corporate tax. Not including any state-mandated levels or thresholds. Costs are annualized. Source: U.S. Dept. of Commerce

Conclusion

As you can see by the above chart, the West took low honors for corporate income tax for all U.S. regions, followed by the American South. However, the West's average is skewed somewhat because three states in the West (Nevada, Washington, and Wyoming) don't have a corporate income tax. The South (Texas) and the Midwest (South Dakota) are the only other regions with a state devoid of corporate income tax. Every state in the Northeast charges a corporate income tax, with the lowest tax rate of 6.215 percent belonging to Maine. Conversely, Connecticut, with 10.5 percent, has the highest state corporate income tax rate in the nation. With all states devoid of corporate tax thrown out of the equation, the previous chart also shows a regional corporate tax average rate based on an average tax paid for companies grossing $10 million. This gives the South a further advantage in net operating costs.

Regional Construction Costs

While many communities throughout the U.S. offer incentives relative to the costs incurred in building a factory or a warehouse facility, few of those programs will directly affect the cost of the

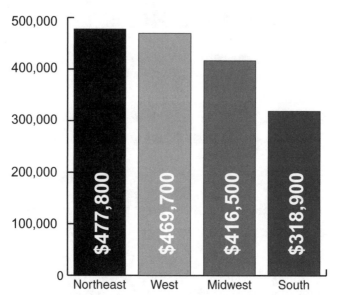

Average Regional Construction Costs
for 100,000-Square-Foot Tilt-Up Concrete Structure

Note: Average cost based on building a 100,000-square-foot structure in a suburban location in the top 10 markets of each region. Taxes, insurance, and maintenance over five-year period included in total cost.
Source: *2001 Comparative Statistics of Industrial and Office Real Estate Markets*

structure itself. Most of those incentives deal with other infrastructure improvements such as roads, sewers, and the like.

The following profiles the average cost of building a concrete wall tilt-up factory or warehouse in the four regions of the U.S. Regional figures were tabulated by averaging the cost of building the facility in a suburban location in the 10 largest markets of each region. The total cost indicated is based on a 100,000-square-foot facility. The total cost includes average regional real estate taxes, insurance (fire and liability), structural and roof maintenance, and common area maintenance expenditures on the building for five years. The cost does not include any equipment in the facility.

Conclusion

By studying the above chart, clearly there is a big difference in the cost of building a 100,000-square-foot facility in the Northeast, West, and Midwest versus the South. On average, the most expensive U.S. markets in which to build such a facility are New York, Boston, Detroit, Minneapolis, and San Jose. The least expensive places to build in the 40 largest U.S. markets are Tampa, Jacksonville, Memphis, Columbus (Ohio), and Salt Lake City.

Cost of Leasing Existing Facilities

For most of this case study, where applicable, we have used the top 10 markets in each U.S. region to find an average expenditure for each region. For the sake of variety and fairness, let's find an average cost for each U.S. region in leasing existing warehouse or factory facilities by using lease costs found in smaller markets. We'll take the same 100,000-square-foot facility and find an average annual net lease based on lease averages found in five small markets representing each region.

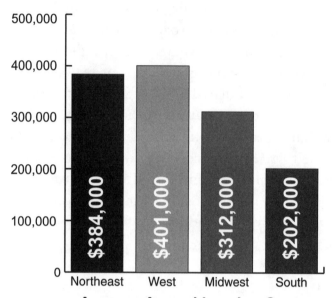

Average Annual Leasing Costs
for 100,000-Square-Foot Warehouse/Factory

Source: 2001 Comparative Statistics of Industrial and
Office Real Estate Markets

Northeastern markets used in the study include Buffalo
(NY), New Haven (CT), Syracuse (NY), Portland (ME), and
Harrisburg (PA). Representatives of the West include Colorado
Springs (CO), Stockton (CA), Tacoma (WA), Medford (OR), and
Reno (NV). Charleston (SC), Chattanooga (TN), Monroe (LA),
Fort Smith (AR), and Corpus Christi (TX) represent the South
and Grand Rapids (MI), Fort Wayne (IN), Des Moines (IA),
Lansing (MI), and Omaha (NE) are representing the Midwest in
this study.

As you can see by examining this chart, the South is your low
price leader again. Of the markets used in this study, Monroe

(LA) is far and away the cheapest place to lease a warehouse or factory, followed by Fort Smith (AR) and Corpus Christi (TX) in the South, and Fort Wayne (IN) in the Midwest.

It should be noted that there is a substantial range in pricing of such real estate and that many factors impact your final rate. They include but are not limited to customization, age of facility, favorable location factors proximate to specific cities and interstate highways, type of construction, expandability, and an adequate infrastructure for expansion to name just a few.

Final Conclusion

So let's tally these costs up. After five years of operating a 100-employee, 100,000-square-foot manufacturing facility that's grossing $10 million in revenue annually, payroll, workers' comp, unemployment insurance, state corporate taxes, and your building are going to cost you $33,501,240 in the Northeast. On average, you're going to pay $28,791,935 for those same expenses in the West and $28,745,355 in the Midwest. But in the South, those expenses are only $24,910,005 after five years.

In other words, by opting for a Southern location for your company, you'll save $8.6 million in five years when compared to the Northeast, $3.9 million over the West, and $3.8 million when compared to the Midwest. It's your money!

Whether you are a business owner, CEO, or an individual looking to lean your career ladder elsewhere, there is certainly a compelling case for you to consider the South. These numbers, coupled with job growth trends, show why the American South will be "where the action is" for the next few decades.

As I am sure you have realized, volumes could be written on this equation of savings as it relates to your particular industry or niche. Further variables may include factors such as the geographic location of particular states, large or small city, metro or rural, proximity to certain transportation outlets, incentive programs, access to training and educational facilities, etc. These variables will depend somewhat on the skill and negotiating ability of the company decision maker as well. In conclusion, the dollar savings shown below are general in nature but an astute company or negotiator could greatly improve the general financial outcome based upon the needs of their company or client.

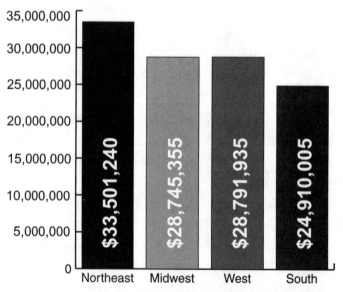

**Average Five-Year
Operating Costs by Region
for a 100 Employee Manufacturer**

eleven

Five of the Most Important Reasons You Should Expand Your Business to the South . . .

or if you are an individual, why you should consider a company in the South for employment

Based upon my research I believe that it would be difficult if not virtually impossible to find a single economic study done in the last two decades that could show any states in the Northeast or Midwest to have a better business climate than any Southern state. I am sure that there are individual exceptions to this based upon specific "company retention" recruitment efforts for particular industry segments, but the list of *Southern advantages* is long, growing fast, and most importantly, COMPELLING!

If you own or operate a business or are just looking for a better career opportunity, I've come up with five overriding reasons (in addition to cost savings) why you should take a closer look at the American South for your career or business. As you will see, all of these reasons are supported by absolute fact, not conjecture or opinion.

#1. Predominance of Right-to-Work

The South is the leading region in terms of Right-to-Work laws and their many advantages.

While lower operating costs may be the most important advantage of doing business in the South, there are certainly many other bottom-line attractions that help make the region the most active economy in the U.S. Officials representing the slew of automakers that have built large assembly plants in the South over the last 25 years will likely point to "Right-to-Work" laws that are on the books in 13 Southern states.

Those automakers, almost all of which are foreign, have recognized that the cost of producing automobiles in more traditional areas, such as Detroit, is prohibitive. Avoiding higher labor costs, oftentimes fueled by organized labor unions in "Rust Belt" states, made the top of the list when it came to site search factor concerns to these foreign automakers. With the landing of Toyota, BMW, Honda, Nissan (two plants), Mercedes, and Hyundai, etc., the "Southern Automotive Corridor" was born. These auto giants have discovered that the vast majority of states in the South have Right-to-Work laws on the books.

Right-to-Work legislation basically means that no person can be denied the right to work because of membership or non-membership in a labor union. It also means that workers cannot be forced to pay union dues, collective bargaining fees, or any other "in lieu" fees in order to keep their jobs. In Right-to-Work states, union membership also cannot be a condition of obtaining or continuing employment. Union membership is not prohibited in Right-to-Work states; it simply means that individual workers can choose whether they want to join a union or not.

The fact that workers have the freedom of choice as to whether or not to join a union that is organized at their place of work may be the most important facet of Right-to-Work legislation. Freedom of choice is what this country is all about. And after the events of 9/11/01, freedom in general has become a supremely important fact of American life. Ultimately, fewer unions means more freedom for employers and fewer labor strikes that could halt production or stifle productivity.

While many important factors go into choosing the most profitable business location, some will argue there isn't a single one more important than the inclusion of Right-to-Work legislation. "Having Right-to-Work laws in place is not the No. 1 factor in a deal. It's not even No. 2," said Charles Kimbrough, a recruiter for the Office of Business Location, a department within the Oklahoma Department of Commerce. "But it could be the No. 1 thing that gets you kicked off the list from the beginning. I've found that many companies that are looking to expand or relocate, give direct orders to their site consultants not to include states that don't have Right-to-Work laws," Kimbrough said.

Bob Goforth, a well-known national site consultant, agrees. "When a company begins a search, the search criteria checklist usually has two columns: needs and wants," Goforth said. "The needs would basically be the absolutes of a particular location and the wants would be things that would be nice to have if they can get them. More often than not, Right-to-Work will be found in the needs column. In other words, for many companies, if you're not a Right-to-Work state, you don't play in the game."

If, according to Goforth and Kimbrough, hundreds of site-searching companies and their consultants eliminate non-Right-to-Work states from the beginning that would naturally translate into more jobs being created in Right-to-Work states. The statistics solidly back up that theory. According to the U.S. Department of Commerce, between 1977 and 2001 Right-to-Work states gained more than 800,000 manufacturing jobs, while states with compulsory unionization lost almost 2 million manufacturing jobs. Talk about staggering statistics and conclusive proof.

Furthermore, according to U.S. Census Bureau statistics, non-Right-to-Work states posted an average population growth rate of 10.61 percent between 1990 and 2001. Right-to-Work states experienced an average population growth of 18.43 percent during the same period. Also, the four non-Right-to-Work states (Missouri, Kentucky, West Virginia, and Maryland) in the South have grown an average of just 7.65 percent since 1990. In contrast, the remaining 13 Southern Right-to-Work states grew their populations by 15.28 percent since 1990, doubling the population growth of their non-RTW Southern brethren.

There's no question that more jobs are being created in Right-to-Work states than in non-RTW states. In fact, our figures show that between 1985 and 2001, nearly as many jobs have been created in the 13 Southern Right-to-Work states than were created in the other 37 states combined.

Let me repeat this statistic because it's so significant—nearly AS MANY JOBS WERE CREATED BETWEEN 1985 AND 2001 IN THE 13 SOUTHERN RIGHT-TO-WORK STATES THAN THE OTHER 37 STATES COMBINED. (Source: Bureau of Labor Statistics)

And there's more evidence to support the attractiveness of Right-to-Work. Dr. James Bennett of the Nobel Prize-winning economics department at George Mason University has studied cost-of-living adjusted household incomes for metropolitan areas in Right-to-Work and non-Right-to-Work states. According to his study, median spendable household income for metro areas in Right-to-Work states is $2,333 higher than in non-Right-to-Work state metros.

Here are some other numbers to consider:

▶ Since 1977, personal income in Right-to-Work states has grown almost 25 percent faster compared to non-Right-to-Work states.

▶ Nine of the top ten states showing the largest growth in manufacturing employment from 1993-1998 were Right-to-Work states.

▶ The 22 Right-to-Work states have had lower unemployment rates than non-Right-to-Work states in all but four years between 1978 and 2001.

▶ Gross State Product (GSP) in Right-to-Work states grew by 38 percent from 1992-1999, while GSP grew by 29 percent in the same period in non-RTW states.

Certainly makes you wonder why any state government in a non-Right-to-Work state would continue to place such a legal bondage on their residents, their income, and their families.

#2. Quality of Labor

Looking for people who will work harder and smarter? Take a closer look at the American South.

For most of its existence the South has relied on an agrarian economy. While that is not the case today, an interesting by-product of the South's agrarian past is being discovered by the record number of companies that have chosen to invest in the region. It is the quality and integrity of the region's labor.

Employers cite the South's agricultural roots as the basis for an outstanding work ethic. Independent thinking derived from the farm mentality of "I've got to fix it myself or it won't get fixed" contributes greatly to the Southern work ethic. That work ethic logically leads to lower levels of absenteeism and turnover and higher rates of productivity. It also means fewer workers' compensation claims.

In fact, you will find incredibly low workers' compensation incidence rates in the South. One recent study done in 1998 indicates that average incidence rates across Dixie are about three percent, a fraction of the seven-plus percent that is the U.S. average.

Absenteeism rates also stand out when comparing the South's workforce to other U.S. regions. A recent university study shows that on average, you'll experience about a 2.6 percent absenteeism rate with a rural South workforce and about a 3.2 percent rate in Southern metros—consistently lower than other regions.

To further point out the dedication workers in the South have to their jobs and companies, you only have to look at the example of Vanity Fair. The apparel company, like many other apparel companies in the rural South, has closed domestic plants and moved them to China and elsewhere outside the U.S. In

1996, Vanity Fair announced it would close a plant in Alabama, putting 500 people temporarily out of work. The company announced that it would provide severance for its 500-employee workforce for one year—plenty of time for someone to decide they wanted to file a workers' compensation claim. The company did not have a single claim filed. Southern workers remained loyal to the company (and were not vindictive) even though they had lost their jobs.

#3. Experience, Economic Development Programs, and Incentives

In the early and mid-twentieth century, the federal government helped create incentives to boost the nation's worst economy. Although it seems like a distant memory, the owner of that "worst economy" was the South. As explained earlier, the South is now by far the nation's and possibly the world's most vibrant economy.

It was in the South that economic development as it's practiced today was invented. This invention was "patented" soon after World War II. Back then, the first incentives designed to attract industry were conceived. At the time, economic development wasn't practiced with any conviction in other U.S. regions. There was no reason for it to be practiced. Times were good in those regions and no federal programs of any significance were in place to boost the economies of the Northeast, Midwest, or West.

As for the South, it still benefits from a tremendous head start of about 30 years in the economic development game when compared to other U.S. regions. The wealth of experience held by state and local economic development agencies in the South has resulted in aggressive measures to attract industry and to close corporate deals seamlessly.

As for Southern state incentives, they remain widely available, more than any other U.S. region. Today, these incentives are also accountable. They are intelligently designed to steer corporate deals to state regions that need the jobs the most, which are often rural areas. Along with these incentives, Southern states also offer tailored financing programs designed to keep their companies profitable.

To exemplify this point, I examined the types of incentives offered by three Southern states: North Carolina, Arkansas, and South Carolina. Along with a wealth of financing-assistance options such as bond and low-interest loan programs for businesses, North Carolina offers job tax credits to companies creating jobs in the state as well as a business energy improvement program to enhance infrastructure. Arkansas offers an Enterprise Zone program (generally a lower taxed, disadvantaged area), a rebate program, and a variety of specialized incentives. Meanwhile, South Carolina brings job tax credits, property tax credits, sales tax exemptions, and tax abatements to the incentive table.

The lists of incentives I have given for these states are by no means exhaustive. Every state in the South stands ready to reward investment and job creation with cost-saving benefits for you. These incentives are fluid as the Southern states continually strive to outdo each other and to stay on the cutting edge in the incentive game. For the latest details on how you can profit from Southern incentives, visit the Web sites for the commerce/economic development agencies of each state. Or better yet, you might want just pick up the phone and give these folks a call. Customization is the name of the game and chances are good that a state in the South will tailor a package to suit your unique needs.

#4. Where the People Are

Historically, the United States has experienced four distinct waves of immigration to its regions. First, it was the Northeast. Companies found profitability by sticking their flags in the ground over 200 years ago in the most populated areas, which at the time were Philadelphia, New York, and Boston. This simple strategy proved as effective then as it still does today: take your business to where the most people are. That is how you will find the best labor resources and the most customers.

After many years of Northeastern domination, the Midwest experienced its own successful corporate immigration run. Areas around Chicago, Cleveland, Pittsburgh, and Detroit saw companies, especially heavy manufacturers, grow at astounding rates. These companies in the Midwest had followed the people. It was and still is a simple, sound strategy. Later, California got in on the act as its population boomed and companies followed.

Today, however, population immigration statistics are virtually a Southern affair. In the late 90s, for example, U.S. Census Bureau figures show that the South was the only U.S. region with a positive net internal migration (excluding foreign immigration).

Another interesting point is that two economic downturns in America, ironically right after the turn of two decades in 1980-1981 and 1990-1991, saw residents in the Northeast and Midwest pack up and leave in droves for the South and West. In 1980-1981 for example, 706,000 people left the Northeast, giving that region a negative 242,000 net internal migration. The Midwest saw over one million people leave during the same time, giving the Midwest a negative 406,000 net internal migration total. Even during this time of economic struggle, the South saw positive net internal migration of half a million people. In other words, a strong national economy makes even a high cost area look attractive to companies and families. However, the South shows its real strength when the economy slows. The subtle, underlying fundamentals that work so diligently for the South's success every day kick into overdrive when the national economy slows by highlighting the advantages of a low-cost producer region.

In the 1990-1991 recession, nearly a million people packed up and left the Northeast, while 797,000 left the Midwest. During that time, the South saw a positive net immigration total of 433,000 residents, while the Northeast saw a net loss of 585,000.

The fact that so many people migrated to Dixie from the Northeast and Midwest during two significant economic downturns indicates that the business climate even during tough times is less tough in the South. Why else would people be leaving in such large numbers to head south? This highlights the simple fact again that a good national economy somewhat manages to mask the success of the South by partially hiding the failures of other areas.

You cannot have economic growth without a critical mass in terms of population. Companies follow the people, who are the customers and potential employees. As we have stated, the most incredible achievement and substantial advantage for companies considering a change is in the fact that the South is now home to DOUBLE the NUMBER OF PEOPLE found in the Northeast.

Just 50 years ago, the Northeast and South had nearly identical population numbers. Now, more than 107 million people live in the South (in the 17 SEDC states). No other U.S. region (even the Northeast) can account for more than 65 million. Where the people are, commerce occurs. That's been the case in America since the settlement at Jamestown.

#5. Low Business Failure Rates

All of these Southern advantages create one unique and important result: businesses fare better in the South than in other regions of the U.S. There is no better way to judge a state or region's business climate than to compare the number of business starts in a region with the number of business failures. This is where the rubber meets the road. It makes sense that this information should have a profound effect on where you choose to operate your business. In 1998, for example, there were 166,740 business starts in the United States. During the same year, there were 83,384 business failures. As you can see, for every two business starts, one business failed in this country in 1998. I wish we could include more current information, however 1998 was largely unaffected by the recent economic slowdown and more recent numbers were not finalized in some cases.

Looking at the figures on a regional basis, the following chart clearly indicates that more businesses are started in the American South than any other U.S. region. The South also has the lowest rate of business failures. The Northeast places second best in the ratio of business starts to business failures and the Midwest runs right along with the national average. Alarmingly, in the West, for every ten business starts, eight go under. (The 1998 figures for the West may be slightly affected by the early signs of the tech bubble bursting.) The business failure rate in the West, in fact, tends to increase dramatically during a recession.

The numbers don't lie. If you want to succeed in business, you are statistically more likely to succeed in the South.

History also shows that the South has a lower rate of business failures compared to incorporations. The year 1998 was far from

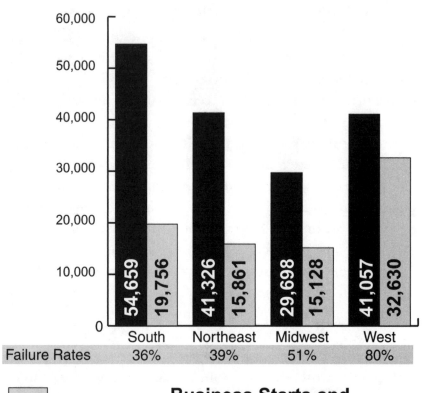

**Business Starts and
Business Failures By Region**
1998

being a "flash in the pan." To prove this point from a historical perspective, the 1992-1994 figures are on the following page:

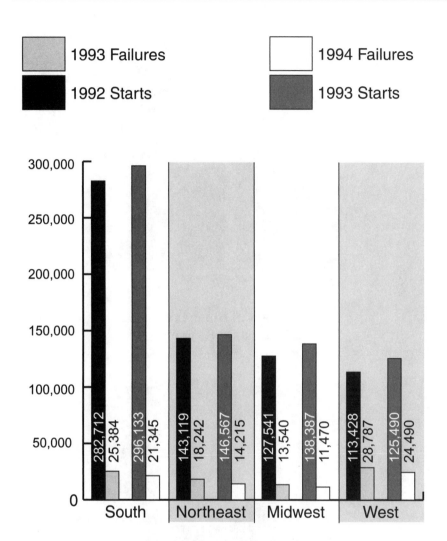

**Business Starts and
Business Failures By Region**
1992-1994

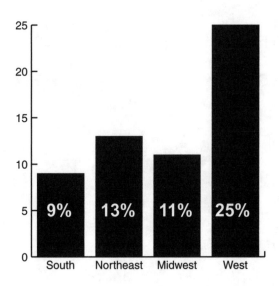

**Percent of Business
Failures By Region**
1992

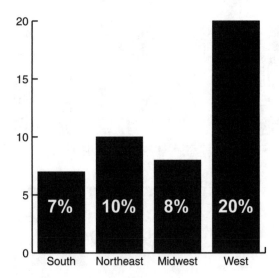

**Percent of Business
Failures By Region**
1993

twelve

Quality of Life Does Matter!

In case no one has mentioned it, you will LOVE living in the South!

True, it has been busy outpacing the rest of the nation, economically speaking, but in many ways the South is still a world all its own. Hospitality, lower living costs, natural beauty, and a sense of history all add up to enjoyable and easy living.

As I have already highlighted, the South has changed dramatically in the last 50 years. Now, grand porches with rocking chairs and tall glasses of sweet tea peacefully coexist with skyscrapers and suburbs. Despite the changes, the swamps of Louisiana and South Florida are still exotic—full of alligators, armadillos, and egrets. The azaleas and rhododendrons of Georgia and the Carolinas are still as gorgeous. The magnolias of Mississippi are still magnificent. Texas is still as proud and Charlie Daniels still puts Southern pride to words most eloquently. The quality of life is still outstanding and improving to boot!

If you own or operate a business, quality of life will directly and indirectly impact your bottom line. In fact, it should be one of your top determining factors in site selection. Your company's capacity to operate profitably hinges on your ability to attract and retain top talent. Talented people flock to places where they can enjoy life.

If you are searching for the best place to put down roots, lifestyle quality should be a high priority. Living where you can play near work simply makes life better, and so does finding a great place to raise a family. Affordable housing, elbow room, and plenty of recreational opportunities make the South a superb choice.

Even if all other factors were equal (and in case you've been sleeping through the previous chapters, they are NOT), the South's qualities combine to make it a region where living and working are truly enhanced.

From my vantage point, the South's distinctive charm and easy living have played big parts in its population explosion. And the boom has resonated throughout the region. Mega markets have sizzled in the past decade. Hot corridors stretch from Nashville to Orlando to Raleigh-Durham, where parts of those metro areas grew at least 50 percent from 1990-2000, according to data from the 2000 U.S. Census. Even tiny places in the region—Tunica, Miss., Bentonville, Ark., and Wakulla County, Fla.—grew at double-digit rates. OK, OK . . . Wal-Mart and gambling had something to do with this but in the South home-grown opportunities become a reality on a daily basis.

"There are a lot of people who have come from the Northeast to Atlanta and Raleigh-Durham (and other places across the South) for the booming economies, high-tech industries and the cost of a (reasonably priced) house," explained Noah Pickus, associate professor at the Terry Sanford Institute of Public Policy of Duke University.

Retirees in particular have been lured by the lifestyle offered in the South. Over the last few decades, Dixie has seen a huge retiree influx, becoming one of America's top retirement destinations. According to AARP (formerly known as the American Association of Retired Persons), researchers including Gordon DeJong, Penn State professor of sociology and demography, half a million older Americans move from one state to another each year. A high percentage of these individuals continue to flock to Florida, but increasingly are considering other Southern states such as South Carolina, North Carolina, Alabama, Mississippi, and Tennessee.

For Americans in the twenty-first century, retirement doesn't just mean playing bingo anymore. Factors like the number of golf courses, sunny days, and good restaurants, neighborliness, low crime, clean air, quality health care, and efficient transportation are all hot-button issues. Many areas in the South, from the mega markets to the small ones, excel in these categories.

Among the rich rewards that retirees will discover in the South are a warmer climate to reduce arthritis pain and similar ailments; improved economic security through the lower cost of living; and a warm, comfortable, environment. Sometimes just the helpful nature of the Southern culture can be extremely valuable for a senior citizen needing assistance of any kind.

Family ties are also drawing retirees to the South. As the population center of the U.S. moves further south as well as west (see map), statistically more of their children and grandchildren have already come in pursuit of a better job and a better life. Older Americans will naturally follow.

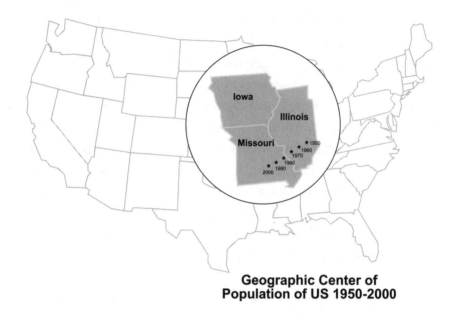

**Geographic Center of
Population of US 1950-2000**

Organizations such as AARP, publisher of *Modern Maturity*, suggest that recent years have brought more opportunity for retirees to head to their dream locations (many of these in the South). These older Americans are living longer and enjoying more prosperity than in past generations. Meanwhile, younger Americans are recognizing the benefit of moving and getting "settled" now where they want to retire later. This from an individual's perspective allows more time to make good friends and develop social connections before entering old age.

The South's low cost of living is perhaps the leading factor in its standout lifestyle quality. A multiplier effect, which occurs through these lower costs, means that Southerners can afford better housing, more leisure time, and more disposable income. In other words, a greater number of people can afford to live the "good life." Even mid-level managers can afford to live an executive lifestyle.

The last four decades have seen the rise of a new middle class. Perhaps nowhere is this statement truer than in the South. By the 1960s, the rising economic tide created scores of new professional jobs such as teacher, accountant, college professor, loan officer, computer programmer, and manager. Sociologists Earle and Merle Black have argued in *Politics and Society in the South* that nearly 60 percent of white Southerners and nearly 30 percent of black Southerners belonged to the middle class by 1980.

Now, let's compare apples to apples:

▶ If you earned $100,000 a year in Birmingham, Mich., you would only have to earn $65,542 to enjoy the same standard of living in Birmingham, Ala.

▶ Moving from Morristown, N.J., to Morristown, Tenn., you would only have to earn $68,981 to enjoy the same lifestyle that required $100,000 in New Jersey.

▶ Most amazing, you would only need HALF of the money in Danville, Va., versus Danville, Calif., to experience the same standard of living ($100,000 in California versus $50,098 in Virginia).

All of this according to homefair.com's salary calculator, second quarter 2002 figures. I encourage you to check out this Web site yourself and promise you'll be amazed at how the cost of living in Southern cities is consistently less than other parts of the nation.

As one couple from the Northeast put it so eloquently, "We love New York, but it's no place to retire unless you're very rich."

If one of the nation's high-tech MSA's is a better fit for you or your business, compare San Francisco to Austin. If you earned

$100,000 in San Fran, you would only need $60,735.12 in Austin to equal your living standard—that's $39,264.88 less!

On average, a family's housing cost totals 28 percent of its annual household budget. So, saving money on housing translates into a dramatically higher disposable income. You will also save money on real estate taxes because of the difference in assessed values.

Contributing to the lower cost of living in the South is highly competitive housing costs. Looking at average home prices for a 2000-square-foot home in similar-sized markets:

- ▶ You would pay $406,000 in Los Angeles, but only $262,000 in Atlanta.
- ▶ You would pay $314,000 in Danbury, Conn., but only $102,000 in Columbia, S.C. (Yes, that's right, you could buy three houses for the price of one! How about a vacation home, too?)
- ▶ In Hackensack, N.J., that 2000-square-foot home would cost you $236,000 while in Clarksville, Tenn., it would only cost $126,000.

Home prices are based on the Web site Monster.com, 2002 figures.

A larger home for your family, a larger yard in a great neighborhood—all for less money. That's what you'll find in the South.

The following figures reflect cost of living in several of the nation's markets taking into account the price of groceries, housing, utilities, transportation, health care, and miscellaneous goods and services.

As the above Cost of Living charts indicate, the South is the only region that is below the U.S. average (at 95.8 percent). Along

COST OF LIVING IN SELECT MARKETS OF THE WEST
U.S. AVERAGE = 100; WEST AVERAGE = 110.5

COST OF LIVING IN SELECT MARKETS OF THE MIDWEST
U.S. AVERAGE = 100; MIDWEST AVERAGE = 101.5

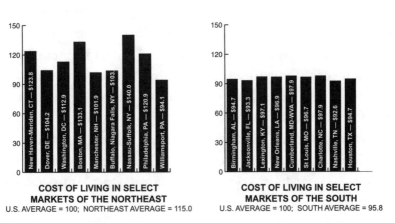

COST OF LIVING IN SELECT MARKETS OF THE NORTHEAST
U.S. AVERAGE = 100; NORTHEAST AVERAGE = 115.0

COST OF LIVING IN SELECT MARKETS OF THE SOUTH
U.S. AVERAGE = 100; SOUTH AVERAGE = 95.8

Source: U.S. Census Bureau 2001, cities selected at random.
Excludes New York City at 235.2

with this lower cost of living, the South also offers an abundance of sports, entertainment, and family-friendly enjoyment. From its mountains and coasts to its prairies, the South offers something for everyone.

Broad sandy Atlantic and Gulf Coast beaches (within a day's drive from virtually anywhere in the South) are magnets for water sports and quiet strolls. The region's national parks such as the Blue Ridge Parkway (N.C., Va.)—the most visited national park—attracts nearly 20 million annually according to the National Parks Service. The Great Smoky Mountains (Tenn.), Shenandoah (Va.), Big Bend (Tex.) and numerous others, plus state parks are havens for nature-based activities and programs. A huge number of historic sites tell compelling stories of the past, from the South's colonial roots and fight for secession to its struggle for civil rights and emergence as America's most progressive region.

Larger cities and downtowns across the South foster cultural events, museums, wonderful restaurants, symphonies, and other world-class entertainment. For example, markets like Orlando and Nashville are MSA's for tourism and entertainment. Atlanta boasts successful professional sports teams, state-of-the-art sports facilities including the Atlanta Motor Speedway, and some of the world's most prestigious sporting events.

Meanwhile, colorful festivals celebrating everything from peaches to okra lure visitors to explore small-town charm. Centuries-old gardens, scenic mountain vistas, and rural towns are strung like jewels all across Dixie.

Many of the South's manmade attractions draw up to half a million visitors each year.

Alabama offers the U.S. Space and Rocket Center (Huntsville) and the Birmingham Zoo. Kentucky is proud of its Newport Aquarium, Kentucky Horse Park (Lexington), and Louisville Zoo. More than 2,000 animals plus exotic-plant exhibits await visitors at South Carolina's Riverbanks Zoo and Botanical Garden (Columbia). St. Louis offers its trademark arch and Houston its Johnson Space Center.

Asheville, N.C., is home to America's largest mansion open for tours, the Biltmore Estate. In Tennessee, Memphis keeps

Elvis' memory alive at Graceland, and showcases wild animals at its Memphis Zoo. Gatlinburg offers a wide range of outdoor and indoor fun through all four seasons. Chattanooga boasts one of the nation's best aquariums. In Williamsburg, Va. and Charleston, S.C., visitors can check out the incredible history of our nation's early days.

Of course, there's Orlando, with Walt Disney World, Universal Studios, Cypress Gardens, and more than 60 other attractions not to mention the Space Center, Cape Kennedy, and Port Canaveral.

That brings us to GOLF. In the South, thousands of the world's top courses are neatly packaged in one region. Most places in the region, golfers can play 365 days a year!

Vacation hotspots abound in the South, too. Located not far from trendy Miami, Fort Lauderdale attracts vacationers with prominent golf courses, sandy-white beaches, and great dining and shopping. The Outer Bank Connection, off the coast of North Carolina, offers championship fishing, uncrowded beaches, and incredible golf courses. Alabama is home to Robert Trent Jones Golf Trail—a major attraction for economic development and tourism.

In South Carolina, Myrtle Beach reigns as the golf capital of the Atlantic Seaboard and America's number-two family-vacation destination. Tiger Woods has called this community "the golf Mecca of the world." The Palmetto State is also proud of charming Charleston, with its many championship golf courses, and nearby Kiawah Island, another great golfing playground (host of the 1991 Ryder Cup). Famous Hilton Head Island, S.C., serves up championship golf as well as miles of unspoiled beaches and numerous family activities. The famous Pinehurst facility with its world renowned #2 Course remains a favorite for the avid golfer. And last but not least, how could we forget one of the hottest vacation spots in the entire South, the Florida Panhandle, also fondly called the "Redneck Riviera."

Some of the most spectacular natural beauty on earth is located in the Southern United States. The mountains of eastern Tennessee, Northern Georgia, western North Carolina, and Virginia are especially blessed with an abundance of national parks and forests, charming villages, and local craft shops. Texas has its Hill Country with German ambiance.

More than four million people annually visit the 3,200-acre Stone Mountain Park near Atlanta, Ga. Its main attraction, often referred to as "the Eighth Wonder of the World," is the largest relief carving on the biggest mass of exposed granite on earth. Mammoth Cave National Park in Kentucky, established in 1941, continues to awe 1.8 million visitors a year with its subterranean wonders.

Along with its other attractions, the South also has a well-earned reputation as a sportsman's paradise. If fishing is your thing, tournament-quality freshwater and saltwater opportunities abound. Southern waters offer everything from largemouth bass and trout to blue marlin and tuna. If you prefer hunting, you can take aim at whitetail deer, ducks, and virtually every form of wild game in between, with your bow or gun.

And then there's the weather. Imagine it for a moment—brutal winters gone. For businesses, a location in the South will undoubtedly mean fewer delays and weather-related closings. In other words—less costly downtime.

For individuals, moving to the South means an opportunity to leave behind most of the snow (and the shoveling). It also means a higher number of days of sunshine each year in many of Dixie's cities. As numerous scientific studies have proven, warmer, sunnier weather can lead to higher energy levels, a better outlook, and increased personal productivity.

We have included a few comparisons of average daily temperature, average days of precipitation, and number of days of snow and ice pellets by city and region within the following charts.

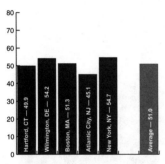

ANNUAL AVERAGE DAILY MEAN TEMPERATURES FOR SELECTED CITIES IN NORTHEAST
IN FAHRENHEIT DEGREES. AIRPORT DATA.
BASED ON STANDARD 30-YEAR PERIOD 1961-1990.

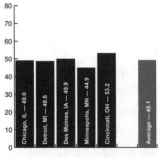

ANNUAL AVERAGE DAILY MEAN TEMPERATURES FOR SELECTED CITIES IN MIDWEST
IN FAHRENHEIT DEGREES. AIRPORT DATA.
BASED ON STANDARD 30-YEAR PERIOD 1961-1990.

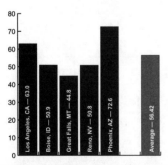

ANNUAL AVERAGE DAILY MEAN TEMPERATURES FOR SELECTED CITIES IN WEST
IN FAHRENHEIT DEGREES. AIRPORT DATA.
BASED ON STANDARD 30-YEAR PERIOD 1961-1990.

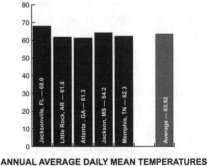

ANNUAL AVERAGE DAILY MEAN TEMPERATURES FOR SELECTED CITIES IN SOUTH
IN FAHRENHEIT DEGREES. AIRPORT DATA.
BASED ON STANDARD 30-YEAR PERIOD 1961-1990.

Source: U.S. National Oceanic and Atmospheric Administration
Cities selected at random. City office data.

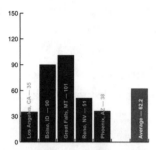

**AVERAGE NUMBER OF DAYS WITH PRECIPITATION OF
0.01 INCH OR MORE—SELECTED CITIES IN WEST**
AIRPORT DATA FOR PERIOD OF RECORD THROUGH 1999.

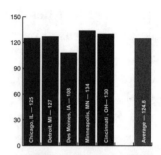

**AVERAGE NUMBER OF DAYS WITH PRECIPITATION OF
0.01 INCH OR MORE—SELECTED CITIES IN MIDWEST**
AIRPORT DATA FOR PERIOD OF RECORD THROUGH 1999.

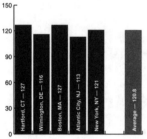

**AVERAGE NUMBER OF DAYS WITH PRECIPITATION OF
0.01 INCH OR MORE—SELECTED CITIES IN NORTHEAST**
AIRPORT DATA FOR PERIOD OF RECORD THROUGH 1999.

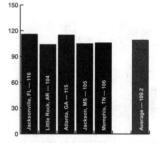

**AVERAGE NUMBER OF DAYS WITH PRECIPITATION OF
0.01 INCH OR MORE—SELECTED CITIES IN SOUTH**
AIRPORT DATA FOR PERIOD OF RECORD THROUGH 1999.

Source: U.S. National Oceanic and Atmospheric Administration
Cities selected at random. City office data.

As positive as previous charts are concerning everyday livability in the South, you cannot discount the value of Southern
hospitality in creating a wonderful quality of life. As a breed,
Southerners are friendly, warm, and welcoming.

In cities across the South, simple "hellos" perplex folks from
elsewhere. You'll still hear "yes ma'ams" and "yes sirs." You'll still
see favors readily extended. Even with the flood of newcomers,
Southern manners have not been extinguished.

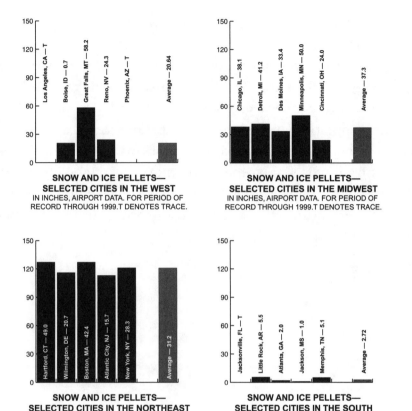

**SNOW AND ICE PELLETS—
SELECTED CITIES IN THE WEST**
IN INCHES, AIRPORT DATA. FOR PERIOD OF
RECORD THROUGH 1999.T DENOTES TRACE.

**SNOW AND ICE PELLETS—
SELECTED CITIES IN THE MIDWEST**
IN INCHES, AIRPORT DATA. FOR PERIOD OF
RECORD THROUGH 1999.T DENOTES TRACE.

**SNOW AND ICE PELLETS—
SELECTED CITIES IN THE NORTHEAST**
IN INCHES, AIRPORT DATA. FOR PERIOD OF
RECORD THROUGH 1999.T DENOTES TRACE.

**SNOW AND ICE PELLETS—
SELECTED CITIES IN THE SOUTH**
IN INCHES, AIRPORT DATA. FOR PERIOD OF
RECORD THROUGH 1999.T DENOTES TRACE.

Source: U.S. National Oceanic and Atmospheric Administration
Cities selected at random. City office data.

On that note and for nearly a decade, Charleston, S.C., has
been recognized each year by etiquette expert Marjabelle Young
Stewart as the nation's most mannerly city. Other Southern markets also have ranked among her top picks recently: Atlanta,
Mobile, Savannah, Memphis, Nashville, and Orlando. Atlanta

was voted the friendliest of 15 major U.S. cities in a Roper poll of recent years.

"Charleston is the role model for the rest of the country," said manners-guru Stewart. "One woman said, 'I make sure I visit there once a year to see a gentleman in action.'"

The population explosion proves it. Americans can't seem to get enough of the South and its exceptional quality of life. So, come on down. Eat some barbeque. Up-size your house. Downsize your budget. Leave your snow shovel behind. Soak in our Southern hospitality. You will transform your life by experiencing our unique Southern spirit.

Predictions, Projections, and Trends

W hat fool would ever want to put in black and white (for all to see and laugh at) a chapter of predictions? P.T. Barnum said that a sucker is born every minute so to prove it in my own case here goes . . . .

Future Opportunities and Future Challenges for the "New South"

A wise person once said that those who do not learn from history are doomed to repeat it. The South, however, has learned profound lessons from its past mistakes and shortcomings. It has made a 180-degree turn from its economic direction of only a generation ago. And in its rise to prominence, the South has proven it can strategically overcome any obstacle on its path to prosperity.

In light of the region's dramatic transformation, I believe that the South has built a strong forward momentum to further accelerate its positive economic direction. The region remains the least unionized and lowest in operating costs, while offering favorable business incentives and rich hospitality. For these reasons, the South of today is fast emerging as a center of high-tech research, manufacturing, and entrepreneurship.

Its economic engine now roaring, the South stands on the brink of opportunity. It can continue shaping itself into the driving force behind America's economic system. With the right elements of opportunity, lifestyle quality, and commitment to business success, the South holds great promise for remaining an economic powerhouse well into the mid-century.

As we have examined the South's past, I believe we also must look forward. This chapter will help us gain perspective on the challenges and opportunities that line the road ahead. Following are a few of my personal projections, predictions, and trends for the South's future.

Prediction 1
The South becomes even more competitive in the world economy

It's a matter of economic balance. Without a doubt, the South has been profoundly affected during the last couple of years of the old millennium and the first few years of the new millennium by the erosion of the U.S. manufacturing base, primarily due to the strong value of our dollar when compared to other major currencies in the world. In the last decade, the dollar experienced continued strength, while the remainder of the world's currencies generally declined. Unfortunately, an overvalued dollar raises the cost of American goods abroad and makes foreign-made goods cheaper and easier to sell in the United States. This has recently been partially corrected by the dollar falling compared to other currencies but this trend needs to be dramatic and sustained. Let's review a few regions of the world in terms of their currency.

The past East Asian financial crisis caused currencies of that region to plummet in value against all major world currencies. With the strength of the U.S. economy, international investors put their assets in the United States, causing the dollar to rise.

Europe, even with its visionary conversion to the euro as common currency, has in general continued its socialistic immoderation and has largely failed to foster entrepreneurial settings for young high-growth companies. This trend dates back more than 30 years with no real change in sight. Also a strain on its economy, Europe is home to an aging population, which is not growing at the pace of the rest of the world. Even with its euro, long-term economic trends for this area are not overly promising.

Japan has continued to experience an economic "hangover" during the 1990s from a massive economic implosion that was building as early as the 1980s. Sadly, I believe that our Japanese trading partners have yet to join reality by facing their economic problems.

The Japanese economy (and thus the yen) has been abnormally weak because the banking and political systems have yet to purge themselves of the previous time of excess. However, the long-term outlook for this country is more favorable, as it begins to slowly cleanse itself of banking immoderation and defaulted loans. As Japan breaks free from the current situation, it is likely the Japanese economic system and currency will be more viable by 2010.

The whole of Asia is now moving toward a mechanized and manufacturing-based economy, driven by extremely low wages. While none of the currencies on the Asian continent are dominant at this point, the economic positions of several countries there are improving. The group as a whole is making its presence known. This trend is helping to stabilize the world economy, but Asia is presently devoid of true strength or leadership.

It should be noted that China's massive population, coupled with its mad dash toward capitalism, have the potential to make this country the largest economic power in the world. In fact, Chinese is projected to be the dominant language on the Web by 2007, according to *The English Place, Ltd.*'s article "How the Internet Changes Economies." China's currency will gain strength, respect, and prominence, even though it is currently tied to the U.S. dollar. The pressure will continue to mount to allow China's currency to float. This will result in a currency not pegged to the U.S. dollar by 2005.

A major fear of U.S. business should include the growing economic threat of China. I've spent some time in Shanghai, China, and have a small enterprise there, and this country is utterly astounding. While on one hand the communists still hold a sizeable amount of power, the people largely ignore the government when it comes to operating small to medium-sized businesses. China is truly a land of small shopowners and entrepreneurs.

The population of the United States generally views itself as capitalistic and entrepreneurial, but it is a totally untold story that China is absolutely the young bastion of entrepreneurial opportunity. It is a land of contrasts. While visiting I noticed on one page of the Shanghai newspaper (English version) a distinct contrast that was evident in three articles: 1) The government announced a joint partnership with an international development firm for the next phase of its financial district (that dwarfs San Francisco's) 2) It was announced that security was being tightened on its screening portal to imprison individuals bringing in pornographic material over the Web (I understand that no such material exists, but the government is making absolutely sure that it doesn't!) 3) A 50-year-old woman was sentenced to death by a firing squad within 60 days of allegedly embezzling approximately $800,000 (U.S.) with no possibility of appeal. China is focused and potent.

What does a decline in the dollar mean for the South? Good news. It means that the erosion of the manufacturing base in the U.S. as a whole will slow considerably, becoming much more gradual. With the dollar gradually falling, the U.S. currency will continue to dominate the world with its strength, though less each year, and will remain a very stabilizing factor in the world economic system. Only on occasion will this trend be broken when economic "flights to safety" (such as extreme currency fluctuations or devaluations) occur or when military action is imminent. As the dollar falls more in line with the rest of the world currency, foreign companies will begin to lose their advantage in the U.S. marketplace. Goods manufactured outside of this country will begin to cost more, enabling our companies to stay competitive AND stay on U.S. soil.

The long-term trend of the dollar easing its value will set the stage for a return to growth of the South's manufacturing sector compared to that of the United States and the world as a whole. This will occur because of a return-to-manufacturing migration from the North and from other high-cost areas driven by the economic realities of competing with the remainder of the world. I believe the South will even have the opportunity to draw back investment that has gone offshore during the recent high-dollar period.

While some manufacturing job loss may continue, I think that the majority of the erosion has already occurred, most even before the economic slowdown of 2001-2002. A high percentage of the remaining companies simply find it more practical to stay on domestic soil. For those companies that continue manufacturing in the U.S., the pressures of a relatively high dollar will continue, driving companies to constantly evaluate how they can lower their manufacturing and regulatory costs. Because the South offers the lowest costs in the U.S., its economic destiny will continue to be extremely positive, particularly in the service sector and in durable-goods manufacturing. And companies that choose to do business in the South will reap financial rewards.

At the same time, the dollar slowly coming into line with other world currencies will keep constant pressure on profit margins and expenses of U.S. companies—subjecting them to the "economics of reality." This will further increase the need for efficiency in production and cost-effective operation.

To stay successful, companies electing to stay on U.S. soil will need to move where it's most profitable to operate. Since it offers the low-cost U.S. location, the South will continue to be the wise choice for business growth. The South will lead the nation in creating and maintaining manufacturing jobs. In other words, the South will look more appealing every day as a business location.

Prediction 2
The South shifts its focus from manufacturing to the service sector while creating a more profitable and positive environment for manufacturing companies

Lining up with the national trend, the South will continue to replace some of its manufacturing jobs with service-sector positions. In the United States, service-producing industries (including retail and wholesale trade; transportation and utilities; finance, insurance, and real estate; and government, as well as the service sector itself) account for virtually all employment growth since 1989. Employment in manufacturing grew modestly between 1993 and 1998, but has since fallen, and as of the year 2000 stands nearly a million jobs shy of its 1989 level and nearly 2 million jobs shy of its 1980 level (according to the U.S. Bureau of Labor Statistics). The service sector now employs more than twice as many people as does manufacturing in the U.S. as a whole. Nationwide, service sector jobs increased 22.1 percent from 1991-2001.

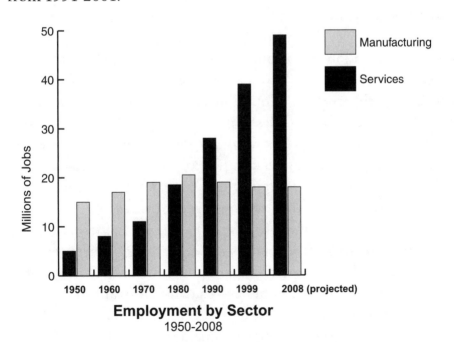

Employment by Sector
1950-2008

The rise of new industries has meant the rise of new jobs, transforming the industry mix. According to Bureau of Labor Statistics Data from 1999, nearly two-thirds of the new jobs created from 1992 to 1999 were managerial and professional jobs.

As indicated in the chart on the previous page, the number of jobs in manufacturing in 1950 was approximately 15 million, and in the services industry was roughly 5 million. By 1980, the service sector began its strong upward trend while manufacturing stayed stagnant and began to decline. By 2008, jobs in the United States service sector will reach more than two and a half times the jobs in the manufacturing sector.

With the nationwide erosion of manufacturing, the roles have reversed with service industries becoming dominant. The enormous growth in the service sector is highlighted by the deterioration of manufacturing.

While increasing productivity per worker in the U.S. has had an impact on job retention, obviously our manufacturing jobs have been in a long downward trend in terms of workforce percentage as the strength of our dollar has exported jobs overseas.

In today's global business climate, manufacturing is far more portable than in 1950. As a result, currencies, taxation, and regulations are now a main deciding factor in where manufacturers choose to produce. Geographic and transportation needs often become secondary in the decision-making process.

The major advantage for the U.S. when it comes to service sector jobs is that most services are virtually immune to export. While certainly the growth of E-commerce will change the world over the next 20 years, I believe that no substantial trend of exporting service jobs will form in the South or across the U.S.

An interesting point is that U.S. manufacturing has had to bear a fairly high degree of taxation and regulation proportionate to its end-result product cost, more so in the United States than in other world economies. America's service industry has not had that disadvantage. In fact, service industries around the globe have been largely on equal footing concerning regulation and taxation, with the exception of labor costs in their respective countries.

Due to the fact that laws are often slow to change, most taxation devised in past decades was oriented toward the production and sale of manufactured goods, U.S. service-industry companies have had a much lighter taxation and regulation burden than manufacturing.

Many decision makers in the tax arena are recognizing that it is fruitless to levy a heavy tax load on manufacturing. Since this sector is becoming more portable companies will simply move away from the area of tax burden, continuing their search for the lowest cost area/country for operation. At the same time, taxation authorities are recognizing that the service sector is less likely to move offshore, and should carry a proportionately higher share of the tax burden.

This dynamic presents an interesting opportunity for elected officials across the South to begin reconfiguring the tax base away from manufacturing and toward service companies. The shift would be dramatic. Up to this point, the South has been over-taxing a shrinking (percentage-wise) sector in the South's economy (manufacturing), largely producing unchanging tax revenues. This inequitable tax situation means that the South's rapidly increasing population is growing faster than the resulting taxes based on goods production.

Shifting some of the South's tax burden to the service industry would automatically produce a seemingly lighter tax load. The growth in the services and tourism sectors is substantially outpacing manufacturing, so the resulting tax would then become elastic and would be spread across a larger tax base. In this scenario, the resulting growth in taxes would be greater than the South's population increase.

It is my belief that a reasonable shift of tax burden away from manufacturing both in the South and in the U.S. as a whole, coupled with the increasing regulatory requirements the rest of the world is beginning to place on industrial growth, will reinforce manufacturing jobs in the South.

The South has considerable room to expand in the service sector. According to The State of the South 2000, in services linked to population—health care, education, and social services—the South still has fewer jobs per 100 people than the nation as a whole. The regional challenge is to shift the balance from low-skill work to higher-skill work as we prepare a workforce for "New Economy" jobs, with services that can deliver the economic boost for the future as when the old economy moved from agrarian to manufacturing. I believe that the South will continue to increase its focus on knowledge-intensive services, and providing a workforce with the necessary education and training.

As of early 2003, manufacturing jobs accounted for just 13.4 percent of employment nationwide. Manufacturing will always be important because it brings money in from outside the region to support service-sector businesses. However, the South must look to sectors outside of manufacturing and the service sector will grow rapidly.

Prediction 3
Migration continues as the South becomes America's "land of opportunity"

Population drives economic development. As the major population migration continues, the South is where the people are going to be.

If you look at projections, according to the U.S. Census Bureau, the South should more than hold its own in terms of population. For example, by 2025, the South (Census South) is projected to have 129 million out of a total 335 million people in the country, holding at roughly 38 percent.

Over the next several decades, I believe that we will continue to see a decline in the Northeast's percentage of national population base. Significant migration and population shifts in the United States will persist, with the South and West continuing to grow.

Forget the West—go South young man!

The influx of new residents in the South recently has also tended to be younger in age than the nation as a whole. The fact that the South is growing in the number of younger, more energetic people has tremendous implications in terms of the increase in available workers ideal for growing companies.

Additionally, better educated and more "risk oriented" people are more likely to immigrate to the South. In fact, demographic studies have shown that highly educated individuals are more geographically mobile than less educated individuals. This influx of younger, well educated go-getters will drive the South as never before. The trend to a lesser degree has been in place for several decades, but in coming years, the South will truly begin to reap the benefits. Momentum will continue to build as the South moves toward a more entrepreneurial-based economy.

As disturbing as it is, I believe that we will see "risk aversion" continue to moderately increase in the nation as a whole.

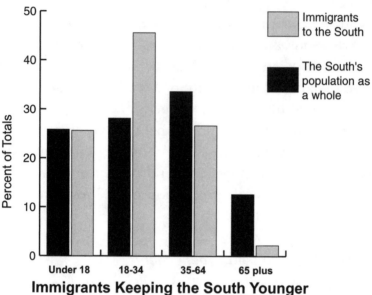

Most immigrants to the South during the 1990s were in the 18-34 age bracket.

Immigrants Keeping the South Younger
Age of immigrants to the Census South, 1990-1998

Meanwhile, "risk-taking" in the South will increase and at the same time the level of success that accompanies such "risk-taking" will increase. As more startup, entrepreneurial companies spring up in the South, their success will likely be due to the younger age, attitude toward independence, and general attitude of migrating individuals toward taking risks. All of this will contribute to the South's increasing economic momentum.

Another major trend is "job churning," the number of new startups and business failures combined, as a share of all businesses. Steady growth in employment masks the constant churning of job creation and destruction, as less innovative and less efficient companies downsize or go out of business, and more innovative and efficient companies grow and take their place. For example, a total of almost 650,000 jobs were added to the U.S. economy between 1997 and 1998, but that was after startup firms had created 6.3 million jobs and failing firms eliminated 5.6 million jobs (jobs were also created and lost from expanding and contracting firms). This churning has hastened as the number of new startups and failures of existing business per year has grown. While such turbulence increases the economic risk faced by workers, companies, and even regions, it is also a major driver of innovation. Some fast-growing states (like Arizona, Florida, Nevada, and Utah) have seen a great deal of churning. In part, this is because fast-growing economies produce more startups, especially in local-serving industries (such as restaurants, dry cleaners, or accountants).

In the past, the South has been able to grow its manufacturing base largely through low-cost labor. However, because of outside influences such as NAFTA, offshore manufacturing production, and the emergence of Asian countries such as China as low-cost producers, the South will continue to undergo job churning. This reduction in low-skill jobs will help to boost the per-capita income in the South as higher skilled jobs replace them. The South will see growth of visionary new industries and companies. In many other areas of the country, the entry-level openings that job churning produces cannot be filled because of a lack of migration and immigration.

The type of job churning happening across many parts of the nation does not enable individuals to climb the career ladder. This is because upper-level jobs are not being created quickly enough. Individuals exchange jobs for a perceived advantage, but in most cases no real long-term gain. By contrast, the South can continue to provide new opportunities in the upper rungs of the job ladder to help its residents find greater job satisfaction and success. This fact is true because of the great number of corporate headquarters, research and development centers, and technology-oriented firms now choosing to locate in the South. This in turn creates upward career movement in the South, so individuals have an opportunity to better themselves at a faster rate.

As it experiences job churning, the South will in fact lose some of its lower-skilled jobs. While this is painful in the short term, the change will undoubtedly bring about positive effects across the region such as raising wage rates for citizens and raising the quality of companies for employees. Southern workers will rise to the challenge. Job churning will bring the South more "New Economy" jobs and move us away from low-wage manufacturing positions. It will also quicken the death of old, outmoded firms and hasten the creation of innovative new companies.

Prediction 4
The South develops its workforce for a knowledge-based economy

As the Southern Growth Policies Board's 2001 Report on the Future of the South explains, "a region's performance in the knowledge economy can rise no higher than the sum of the knowledge of its people." Bearing in mind this principle, workforce development will continue to be one of the most important issues for the South's future.

In the 1990s, an increasing share of companies left behind old ways of organizing work in favor of giving workers more autonomy and the ability to work in self-managed teams. At the same time, many manufacturers have implemented advanced production technologies. Both practices have brought about the need for manufacturers to employ people with a higher level of education.

Why is educating its workforce so important for the South? In the New Economy, which puts a premium on speed and flexibility, an educated workforce is vital to boosting productivity and fostering innovation. Perhaps previous generations only had to work hard to be successful. Today workers have to be educated AND work hard. States with a more educated workforce are better positioned to capitalize on this trend. Twenty-first century opportunity hinges on digital literacy. The South must be ready. As it has transitioned from agrarian to manufacturing, it must now move from manufacturing to a knowledge-based economy.

Fortunately, the South's workforce has proven over time that it has the innate qualities to succeed in the knowledge-based economy. As the onslaught of satisfied and successful Southern companies will attest, Southern workers are generally adaptable, experienced, eager to learn, and ready to change. A high number of college graduates (see chart on the following page for high school and college graduate statistics) in the South are also going back to pursue technical training, readying themselves for the needs of business.

Further, as the Southern Growth Policies Board explains in their report, "The Mercedes and the Magnolia: Preparing the Southern Workforce for the New Economy," the South has outstanding leadership in technical and community colleges; growth in corporate/private universities; a flexible, low-cost system of training; and strong incumbent worker training.

To prepare its workers for the future, I believe that the South will continue to develop what the Southern Growth Policies Board calls a "self-directed" workforce. In this model, the traditional beginning and end to education are a thing of the past. Instead, workers are willing to seek training throughout their careers to update skills.

Degree-Holders
by States in 1990 & 2000

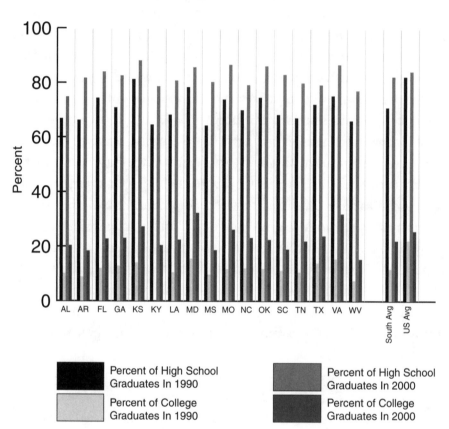

Legend:

Percent of High School Graduates In 1990

Percent of High School Graduates In 2000

Percent of College Graduates In 1990

Percent of College Graduates In 2000

The future South will also begin to take advantage of its under-utilized sources of workers, giving opportunity to all residents and benefiting all businesses. These underutilized groups include the disabled, women, minorities, and retirees.

Prediction 5
Influx of retirees brings necessary capital and expertise for the South's growth

A particularly fascinating trend in terms of population growth is the propensity of early-retiring Baby Boomers to come to the sunny South. This fact means golden opportunities for the region's economy during the retirees' golden years.

For the next few decades, the Baby Boomers will control a vast majority of the wealth in the country. These Southern-retiring Baby Boomers, blessed with wealth and talent, will become either directly or indirectly a major new source of capital infusion in the South, especially in the areas where they live.

With continued capital infusion, the South will no longer be capital starved, as it has been in the past. Capital is imperative for continued forward momentum. With capital being imported at such a rapid rate, the South will, I believe, have its last remaining obstacle to serious growth removed.

Retirees also provide a valuable component for the workforce in the South in that future predictions show a trend that people will keep working beyond traditional retirement age. By 2015, workers 55 and over are projected to comprise nearly 20 percent of the workforce of the nation. The twin attributes of wealth and talent brought by the Baby Boomers to the South will positively impact the region's economic destiny. Capital, coupled with creativity and entrepreneurship, will allow these retirees to create unlimited additional opportunities for the Southern economy.

Prediction 6
The South leads the way in educational reform

The South will continue to strengthen its education system, stretching through its K-12 schools, vocational-technical schools, and community colleges. Admittedly, until recent years, the South has failed to sufficiently address its educational shortcomings. However, the South is increasingly focused on its educational system, is investing more into it, and is committed to sweeping reform. The fact that the South is willing and able to change will become an immense advantage.

Why do I believe that the South will be the leader in improving the American educational system?

1. **The People of the South Themselves Recognize That Their Educational System MUST Change**

    The South is setting goals and seeing vast improvement. Southern leadership is acutely aware that Southern schools are deficient compared to the nation and the world and therefore absolutely must change in order to continue its strong economic momentum.

2. **A Commitment to Benchmarking Students and Teachers Through Testing and Accountability**

    The realization of the need for educational benchmarking through testing has become more prevalent in the South as Southerners understand what has to change. What better way to monitor your progress and overcome perceptions of the "uneducated South" than using national testing as benchmarks? The region will thus be able to address its specific educational deficiencies more directly. In fact, I believe that education's trend toward national testing will be led by the South. Testing will also be a burning issue in the South's political arena for the next several decades. The leaders of the South understand there is no turning back!

3. **Good Ole "Right-to-Work"**

    The South's general lack of unions could become the "ace in the hole" for Southern educational advancement. My belief is that the South will lead the way for the nation's educational change because of the tendency for fewer of the educators to be unionized. As a result of Southerners' independence from unions, they are likely more receptive to change and less entrenched in the old ways of teaching than other areas of the country. Without the "groupthink" that unions sometimes bring, teachers can break free from the shackles of the educational mainstream.

4. **Technology in Schools**

   Not surprisingly, the use of information technology in America's schools is growing. A number of states in the South are furthest ahead in integrating information technology into schools, suggesting that a motivating factor is the desire to establish better connections to information and resources in other parts of the nation and the world. Political leaders in the region will increasingly recognize that the "IT" revolution is important to their future prosperity.

Prediction 7
Contiguous counties around major metropolitan areas will be where the action is in the South

As much of the South during the 50s, 60s, and 70s watched its economy soar, most of the early growth and most celebrated successes occurred in the metro areas. During this time there was a quiet revolution beginning in the semi-rural south, but it seldom gained any notoriety. Indeed if it gained any media attention, it was because of job losses not gains in the less populated counties.

Since the mid 80s, these less populated counties have been gaining more and more acceptance. In fact, I predict that these areas will reflect the new prosperity in the South.

In the past, the counties that are immediately contiguous to established metro areas have largely been treated as bedroom communities and feeders for the growth of the metro area. However, the trend that began in the mid-80s is beginning to bear fruit. These contiguous counties, which are often coming to the forefront in incentive battles to recruit industry, very often are winning out over the metros. While the metro areas have the ability to give larger incentive packages, these contiguous counties many times find that they have advantages in the "quality of life" arena that the metros sometimes are unable to supply. Whether it is the serene setting away from the traffic jams of the metros, better schools, more greenspace, or some other hidden factor, these contiguous counties (tier one counties we will call them) are clearly taking control of the economic destiny of their regions. These tier one counties are also prospering because of leadership that recognizes the value of recruiting the right kind of industry.

In the past, the tier one counties have relied on the larger metropolitan area to supply the majority of the leadership as well as the population mass to be able to attract larger manufacturing entities that paid well. Increasingly, the "quality of life" issue has come to the forefront in a company's location search. As a result, the decision makers of companies are more likely to flee large Northern cities in search of a semi-rural setting that they believe is close enough to a metro to share its advantages, but far enough away to avoid its disadvantages.

The tier one counties, and in some cases the next ring of counties farther out (tier two), are recognizing that they have unique advantages and few of the disadvantages of the old metro-style decaying industry. My prediction is that tier one and tier two counties will become the dominant and assertive economic engines that will drive the South to its next plateau. This will be a result of leadership in these counties recognizing the importance of supplying the "big three brass rings" of a jet-port (a compact version of today's large commercial airports), liquor by the drink, and signature golf communities. If ever there was a secret in recruiting good-paying jobs, the three brass rings are it.

1. A jetport in today's environment is not only the safest way for company executives to travel, but it ultimately becomes the most profitable way. Company leaders are increasingly finding themselves stretched in many directions. And regardless of what other duties they may have, these CEOs frequently have the need to visit their manufacturing facilities. Company leaders can visit three plants in a one long day if done by jet.

   While building jetports within a community can be perceived as a negative, it makes more sense to locate them in industrial parks. So if a community constructs a new industrial park, the ultimate "Mercedes" version would include an airport down the middle of it, thereby taking two potential community negatives and putting them in one locale. This allows industries to face a road and back up to an airport facility. This is the apex of transportation for industry. This plan can reduce community resistance dramatically while more than doubling the success of the industrial park and the immediate use of the jetport. The communities with the vision to capitalize on this recruitment asset will be rewarded by being able to attract some of the most vibrant industries.

2. It is hard to imagine the Bible Belt getting restaurants with "liquor by the drink" (especially if you lived here 50

years ago). But thank goodness, it is widely recognized now that liquor by the drink helps sustain restaurants' profitability. Therefore, this policy is being welcomed in community after community. The issue often becomes a very quiet deciding factor in a community making the last cut of a site selection process. There seems to be an unmentioned perception that communities which have allowed liquor by the drink to attract restaurants are more sophisticated than those that have not.

3. "Golf. It's a four-letter word" mostly said by people preparing to say other four-letter words while playing it. What more can be said about a game that creates legends and closes deals? As a golfer who only plays every couple of years I feel qualified to say (because I am not addicted) that "signature courses" as part of a community package are going to stay a hot ticket. The presence of these courses affords corporate decision makers the security of knowing that their top managers will be able to substantially replace the lifestyle they probably enjoy elsewhere, only in a nicer climate.

The bottom line . . . without these "big three brass rings," (jet-port, liquor by the drink, and a signature golf course) these tier one and tier two counties will always be somewhat dependent on the metros for their success. The cutting edge counties have simply moved ahead. By establishing the "three brass rings" they are putting themselves in the new elite class of sought-after "premier sites." The advantage this generates for the counties with foresight will be their ability to attract the companies and the highest-paying positions with the best benefits.

Generally speaking, these quality companies require premier sites with all three of these "Brass Rings" ready for immediate use. I foresee that these premier tier one and tier two counties will become dominant forces by successfully driving their personal income statistics higher and higher.

Prediction 8
The South becomes practically the
only location for automotive assembly plants

While each of the 800-pound gorillas (better known as foreign automakers) that have stomped through the Southern states has attracted wide attention, I believe that even better times lie ahead for the South. By and large, foreign automakers have had the ability to investigate from a macro-economic level which states afford the best opportunities for them. These assembly plants have predominantly been locating in the South over the last 20 years. The reasons they have chosen the South have ranged from lower costs to labor relations. Most of these investments have been made in Right-to-Work states with reasonable pro-business attitudes and in some cases very heavy incentives.

There has been much discussion in the economic development community as to the recent prices paid per job to attract an assembly plant to locate in certain states. No matter how you pencil it out, the tremendous prices paid per assembly job did not seem to be a good investment for the state. However, this is only a small part of the equation. Factoring in the 20 to 40 tier one suppliers and 100 to 150 tier two suppliers for these assembly plants, the numbers work out with incredible return.

Southern states have gotten wiser about requiring assembly plants to look more closely at the interior part of the state, since the tier one and tier two suppliers need to be within a certain number of miles to service the plant. The goal is for the state to land not only the assembly plant, but also a huge portion of the suppliers. The ripple effect is then felt through the whole state.

The much sought after BMW of South Carolina and Mercedes of Alabama were certainly high profile as well as out-and-out bidding contests. However, for several years prior to these key location decisions, many Southern states were laying the groundwork for automotive success. In many cases it ranged from strengthening Right-to-Work provisions, to reforming business-abusive tort laws and adopting a more progressive political stance.

My prediction as it relates to the automotive industry is simply this. Detroit will wake up with its three domestic manufacturers and realize that the center of gravity of successful automotive plants is in Right-to-Work Southern states. Indeed, the death knell is simply to stay in the "Michigan" mindset. The future of automotive assembly is based upon the facts of the sales trends for domestic-based vs. foreign-based automakers! In my opinion one of the most startling facts is the tendency for these Southern assembly plants to expand within just a few years of opening versus the closing of plant after plant in the North. The center of gravity for the automotive industry has moved south forever.

As we see Ford and Chrysler struggle to maintain their profit margins with GM to soon follow, it is apparent to everybody that the low cost of operation is a major advantage in the South. With these lower costs and the Right-to-Work advantages, the aging assembly plants in the North simply cannot keep up with their Southern counterparts. Obviously this is not a judgment as to whether people living in the North work hard at their automotive assembly plants, it is simply a paradigm shift prompted by a convergence of factors making a Southern assembly plant location the only smart answer.

It may be true that research and development for the "big three" will always be in Detroit. It could be possible that their corporate headquarters may need to be located there also. However, the bottom line is that to refurbish, remodel, or rebuild an assembly plant in the North is simply not going to be any more than a band-aid on a hemorrhage. In order to be competitive, the plants will have to close and begin with a shift in attitude by labor. This will be the only survival option for the "big three." I am a firm believer that the "big three" are going to wake up shortly and begin an exodus. This realization by the big three will happen midway through the first decade of the twenty-first century. By the end of the decade, it will be a foregone conclusion that no automotive assembly plants will be opened outside of the South, except in the most unusual circumstances. This trend will also bring literally thousands of tier one and tier two suppliers to the South, changing the Southern economic destiny forever.

The Final Word . . .

The South is the last frontier for American capitalism. The South has the lowest taxes and the most reasonable regulations, coupled with low unionization. It represents America's last great hope to keep change, innovation, and entrepreneurship alive for the next 200 years. This is not to say that it can't happen elsewhere; it will simply happen in the South far more often.

The South does what we do best and we are what we are. Our culture has produced innumerable changes for over 200 years. Originally, our "nation's best" was in the big cities of the Northeast; then grew to become the powerhouse Midwest; later moving on to the West and California. Now it is the South's turn.

What is the difference this time? We are attracting younger risk takers, the types that have always represented the agents of change. But this time I believe that the key ingredient of this region is its quality of life and general livability. Some would say it is roots, culture, and history. Whatever you believe remember this . . . Our American Constitution explicitly prohibits granting of titles and this spawned the American culture and institutions with the expectation of constant change. Americans have always been receptive to change but increasingly on a national basis, capitalism has been unionized, taxed, or regulated to the point where we are finding it harder and harder to compete in the world economy. The South represents, because of its independence from those shackles of capitalism, America's best hope for competing successfully with the world. The momentum and enthusiasm we are living in the south give us the belief we are too great to dream small dreams.

Finally, I believe that history proves that the South's success is not simply a "flash in the pan." As we embark on the new century and the New Economy, the South, inventor of modern industrial recruitment, is still aggressive and eager to change. Each state is competing against itself to become more appealing for growing companies.

During its "reawakening," the South has gained a renewed dedication to becoming the best possible location for businesses and individuals to thrive. Benefiting from this dedication, now and for the future, are corporate America, small business owners, and anyone in search of a better life. Every year millions of people are discovering the golden opportunities of operating a business as well as living in the American South. You simply can't afford to overlook **the Southern Advantage**.